steaming

great flavor, healthy meals

by Brigid Treloar

PERIPLUS EDITIONS
Singapore • Hong Kong • Indonesia

Contents

Introduction to Steaming

Traditionally, if you mentioned steaming, people would think only of steamed vegetables. But times have changed. The emphasis today is on light, healthy cooking methods that allow the flavor of foods to stand out. Steaming suits this trend perfectly. The natural taste and shape of food is retained, and light flavorings, seasonings and sauces are used to enhance, not to dominate. The taste and aroma of herbs, spices and other condiments are gently steamed into the food.

Steaming comes from an ancient method of cooking that used the stones of hot springs. One of the earliest examples of a steaming utensil is a *hsein*, a two-part bronze steamer (now in the British Museum), thought to have first been used by the Chinese in the eleventh and twelfth centuries B.C. The cooking method of steaming quickly spread from China to Southeast Asia, then to Japan and India, and on to Europe and Britain, each country adding its own flavors and special ingredients and adjusting the methods and cooking times to suit its own cuisine. The Southeast Asian countries used bamboo steamers and woks; the Europeans used steaming baskets and fish kettles, reducing the juices mixed with the steaming liquid to a sauce; the British steamed their suet puddings wrapped in floured cloths; and the Scots their haggis in a sheep's stomach. Steaming was here to stay.

One of the gentlest methods of cooking, steaming suits a wide range of foods and yields subtle, moist and aromatic results. The even heat of the simmering liquid's vapors gently envelops the food resting above in a perforated container, and allows the food to retain most of its natural juices, flavor, color, vitamins and minerals, which would otherwise be lost in the cooking water. The use of fat is unnecessary, making steamed food is light and healthy.

Steaming is a surprisingly easy way to cook, without the need for expensive equipment. So, if you haven't yet tried steaming, follow some of the recipes in this book. You will be pleasantly surprised.

Equipment for Steaming

Many types of equipment can be used for steaming, ranging from the expensive to the extremely cheap. Foods can also be cooked in their own steam without any added liquid. They can be placed in a casserole dish or a saucepan with a tight-fitting lid over low heat, or wrapped into a "parcel" and placed in a steamer. If food is wrapped, allow a little more cooking time.

1. **Steamer baskets and pots:** Stovetop steamers, with one or two handles, come in many sizes, shapes, materials and prices. The steamer basket can be bought separately, or in sets with a base saucepan, but usually there is only one lid for the set. Aluminum, stainless steel, or enamel steaming baskets fit snugly into standard-sized saucepans to steam on the stovetop. (The different bases of saucepans transfer heat differently; the more efficient, the more expensive.) Some steamer baskets have a ridged base that fits a number of different-sized saucepans snugly, allowing no steam to escape. The ridging does mean that the diameter of the base is smaller than the diameter of the top—a disadvantage as some food may have to be overlapped to fit, and could cover all the steam holes. These types of steamer baskets are usually quite deep, which can make it difficult to remove the food after it is cooked.

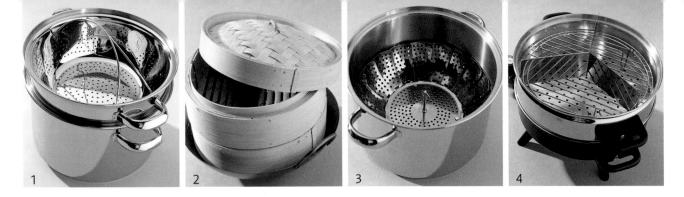

A pasta pot with a deep, perforated basket with handles doubles well as a steamer. The "multifunctional" pot has an additional shallow perforated basket that fits snugly on top as a steaming basket. It's worthwhile to get such a versatile set.

Multitiered aluminum or stainless steel steamer sets, available in Asian stores, are multipurpose. With a base and usually two steaming baskets, they can be used to cook a whole meal. The light-gauge aluminum is not very sturdy; spend the extra money and buy stainless steel.

Although traditionally used to poach whole fish, fish kettles can be used to steam quantities of foods with short cooking times, such as corn on the cob. The perforated tray is very close to the bottom so you will have to refill it often with water.

2. Bamboo steamers: One of the cheapest and most attractive utensils for steaming is the two-level bamboo steamer, available in many sizes from Asian supermarkets and specialty cookware shops. The open-slat base allows steam to circulate easily and efficiently. The lid has an almost perfect design, allowing excess steam to escape through the tightly woven bamboo, with little condensed steam dripping back onto the food. The depth of the bamboo steamer, especially the smaller ones, could be a limitation for some cooking. Alternatively, cover the steamer with foil instead of the lid, or turn another bamboo basket upside down over the food—this will allow extra height—and then cover with the lid.

A 12-inch (30-cm) steamer fits perfectly into a standard 14-inch (35-cm) wok, and easily holds a dinner plate for steaming whole fish. Slower-cooking foods are placed in the bottom level and faster cooking in the one above; also, to even out cooking times, you could change the baskets around during the cooking process. An entire meal can be prepared at once, or the same dish can be cooked in several batches.

A few points to remember when using a bamboo steamer:

- Soak new steamers in cold water for at least 2 hours before first use, to clean thoroughly.
- If there are large gaps between the bamboo slats, place the food on a plate, parchment (baking) paper or leaves.
- If you are lining the steamer, leave some space on the base to allow steam to circulate efficiently.
- Bamboo steamers look good enough to serve from at the table, but should be placed over a plate to catch drips.
- If the lid is a bit loose when cooking, wrap a damp towel around it to stop steam from escaping.

If cooked food is to be left in the steamer for any length of time before serving, place a tea towel under the lid to catch any condensation. To clean a bamboo steamer, simply rinse it in hot water after each use and dry thoroughly before storing in an airy place.

3. Collapsible steaming baskets and steaming plates: Cheap, easy to store, and available in different sizes, collapsible aluminum and stainless steel steaming baskets fold out to fit inside saucepans. Most have a removable handle and small feet. There is not much room for water underneath the baskets, so you should check the water level regularly. To steam small portions in a saucepan, if you are cooking for only one or two, perforated steaming dishes or plates with feet and a handle are very useful. They are available in specialty cookware shops.

4. **Electric steamers:** These two-tiered, plug-in steamers can cook larger quantities of food at once, or even a whole meal. Put meat and fish in the lower steamer and vegetables at the top. A timer reminds you to turn this steamer off, which is good, as it cooks faster than most others. Some even have an alarm that will go off if the water starts to boil dry. For cooks who have everything, there are now built-in steamers just like those restaurants use. They are fast and efficient, but expensive.

5. **Electric rice steamers:** Some Asian countries use what looks like an upside-down bamboo hat that sits over a pot of simmering liquid to steam glutinous rice to perfection. For most people, however, a conventional electric rice cooker is the way to go. Besides cooking rice perfectly, it can be used simultaneously as a steamer. The steaming rack is placed in the cooker with the appropriate amount of water. If no rack is supplied with your rice steamer, use a cake rack, trivet or upside-down bowl. Place food on the steaming rack and cover with the lid, then switch on the cooker. Once the rice is cooked the device automatically switches to the warm cycle; however, the food should be served as close to cooking time as possible.

6. **Do-it-yourself steamers:** If no special steaming equipment is available, simply improvize with what you already have in the kitchen. A metal colander or sieve over a large pot of simmering water—make sure it does not touch the water—can work just as well as the most expensive equipment. Wrap a tea towel around the edge to fill any gaps between the colander and saucepan where steam might escape. If no lid is available, just cover the pan tightly with foil. No metal colander? Place a cake rack, upside-down bowl or trivet in the pot so it is above the level of the water. Put the plate of food to be cooked on top, and cover the pot with a tight-fitting lid or foil.

7. **Couscousières:** The Moroccan couscousière is traditionally used as a casserole to cook vegetables, fish or meat in the base while the couscous is steamed in the perforated top section. It can also be used as a regular steamer, with simmering liquid in the lower section.

8. **Pressure cookers (infusion cookers):** The traditional pressure cookers are now often called infusion cookers, but the principle is exactly the same: pressurized steam in a sealed pan can halve the normal cooking time. Some much-needed safety features have been added to today's pressure cookers. If too much steam builds up, a valve is automatically opened to release it, and the lid cannot be removed until the pressure has dropped. This is a great improvement on old-fashioned pressure cookers, which could cause accidents if the lid was removed before the pressure had dropped. Steamer baskets are an extra purchase, but are very useful, especially for small quantities of food.

Step-by-Step Steaming Methods and Tips

1 Oil the base of a bamboo steamer or steamer basket, or simply line the steamer with parchment (baking) paper or leaves to prevent food from sticking. Do not cover the base completely, as some space must be left for steam to circulate efficiently. For dumplings and buns, you can cut individual pieces of parchment (baking) paper.

2 Place the food to be cooked in the bamboo steamer or steamer basket. Always keep the food about 1 inch (2^1/$_2$ cm) from the sides of the steamer.

3 Partially fill a wok or pot with water and bring to a rapid boil. The base of the steamer should be just above the level of the boiling liquid and should not touch the liquid.

4 Cover and steam until the food is cooked. Occasionally check the water level, adding more boiling water if necessary. Remove the steamer or basket from the wok or pot before removing the food.

Whether you are using the latest in steaming equipment, or a do-it-yourself steamer, there are a few basic tips to remember. One of the most important things to note is that only the highest quality ingredients should be used when steaming food, as steaming accentuates the slightest doubtful odor or blemish.

• If the food is likely to release juices, place it in a shallow bowl or deep plate; the juices can be used as a sauce.
• Steam over medium heat, keeping the water at a rapid boil. To be alerted to a low water level, place 2 or 3 marbles or coins in the base of the steamer. The gentle knocking sound they make in boiling water will stop when the water level drops too low.
• Food that is steamed will be flavorful and succulent, but, unless browned first, it will be pale in color. Simply serve with a sauce or garnish to add color.
• Cooking time can be shortened if the food is cut into small pieces. For even cooking, make sure the pieces are about the same size.
• Cooking is timed from the moment the food is placed in the steamer over the already boiling water and covered. Make sure the lid is firmly in place so that no steam escapes.
• When you steam meat, the steam will cause fat to melt and fall into the boiling liquid, thereby reducing the fat content.

- Steamed whole fish retains its shape better than fish cooked in liquid. However, be careful when lifting it out. Placing a whole fish on parchment (baking) paper or a leaf makes removal easier. Scrunch up the paper around the fish, or leave it on the leaf to serve.
- Parchment (baking) paper and leaves can also be cut to fit under small pieces of food, such as dumplings, allowing steam to circulate efficiently.
- Do not sprinkle salt over vegetables, as it draws moisture out during cooking and may discolor them.
- Layer food according to cooking times, placing the longest-cooking item on the bottom.

The steaming liquid: Water is the most common steaming medium, but stock, beer, wine and other liquids can be used to impart subtle flavors. To make an infusion, bring liquid to a rapid boil and drop in a bunch of fresh herbs; then remove the pot from the heat. Leave to infuse for 20 minutes before reheating to use as the steaming liquid. Flavored steaming liquids can be strained into a small saucepan after the food is cooked, then reduced and used or added to a sauce.

More Steaming Ecoutrements

The recipes in this book require a number of supplies and ingredients that are commonly found in the modern kitchen and easily available in general grocery stores and Asian stores. In the cooking method, kitchen towels, parchment (baking) paper, ramekins (can be substituted with Chinese teacups) and small dishes are also called for, to place inside a bamboo steamer or steamer basket. It's a good idea to have these items handy before beginning a recipe.

Wrappers and liners: Wrapping food and placing it on a heat source is as ancient as cooking itself. While wrapped food takes a little longer to cook, wrapping adds an extra flavor that enhances simple meals, and creates a great presentation. Green leaves such as lettuce, cabbage, grape, and spinach create a flavorsome, edible wrap while banana, palm, lotus leaves and corn husks, though inedible, impart flavor and protect the food and its shape. Both of these types of wrappers can also be used as liners.

Because leaves hold in moisture, leaf parcels reheat well, often have a better flavor the day after being cooked, and are easy to handle. Use string to tie parcels.

Examples of functional wrappers and liners that stop food from sticking, but impart no flavor to food, are aluminum foil and parchment (baking) paper. When using foil, always oil it first and place food on the shiny side. Because wrappers are insulated, allow slightly longer cooking time for wrapped food, or raise the temperature a little so the cooking time remains the same.

Inedible wrappers: Banana leaves, pandanus leaves, bamboo leaves, lotus leaves, aluminum foil, parchment (baking) paper, oven bags.

Edible: Rice paper wrappers, wonton wrappers (square or round), pot sticker (gow gee) wrappers, cabbage leaves, spinach leaves, grape leaves, bean curd sheets, seasoned tofu (bean curd) pouches, crepes, nori (seaweed).

Essential Ingredients

Bamboo shoots are tender but crisp shoots, available in cans or in frozen packets from most stores. Used for texture rather than flavor.

Banana leaves have large, flexible, green, but inedible leaves, used throughout Asia as disposable plates and for wrapping food to be baked or steamed. Available fresh from Asian food stores or frozen and fresh from specialty websites. Best to use within 7 days.

Black dried Chinese mushrooms are strongly flavored so

use sparingly. Soak in hot water for 15–20 minutes to reconstitute. Discard hard stems and squeeze excess water before use.

Bok choy is an Asian green vegetable, also known as Chinese cabbage, with thick white stems and mild-flavored, dark green leaves. Baby bok choy and Shanghai bok choy are also available. All can be substituted in recipes with Chinese broccoli, choy sum, or other leafy greens.

Chili peppers come in many shapes, sizes and colors. Fresh green and red **Asian finger-length chilies** are moderately hot. Available fresh in Asian food stores.

Choy sum is an Asian green vegetable with yellow flowers and thin stems, also known as flowering cabbage. The whole plant can be lightly steamed and eaten.

Coriander leaves are also known as cilantro or Chinese parsley. Available fresh, the roots, stems and leaves are all used in cooking, but as they are strongly flavored, use sparingly.

Dried bean curd skins are the film that forms on top of boiling soy milk; it is dried and sold in sheets as a wrapper,

Fish sauce is a pungent, strong-flavored, salty sauce, extracted from salted fermented fish. It's used to enhance and add depth of flavor to dishes. Flavor and saltiness differ with different brands. Fish sauce from Thailand, called *nam pla*, is commonly available. Don't be put off by the strong fishy smell; there is really no substitute.

Five spice powder is a mixture of five spices of equal parts—cinnamon, cloves, fennel seed, star anise and Sichuan pepper.

Fresh yellow wheat noodles are thick, spaghetti-like noodles made from wheat flour and egg. Substitute fresh spaghetti or fettuccine if you cannot find them.

Glutinous rice or sticky rice is a variety of short grain rice that is more starchy than normal rice when cooked. Two types of glutinous rice are commonly used in Asian desserts: the white grain and the black grain. Glutinous white grain rice is readily available from Asian food stores, while glutinous black grain rice is sold at specialty stores.

Gow gee press is a plastic utensil for making *gow gee,* or dumplings. Available from Asian food stores.

Green onions are also known as scallions, spring onions or sometimes shallots. Green onions have slender stalks with dark green leaves and white bases. They are sprinkled generously on soups and as a garnish.

Hoisin sauce is sweet, thick, Chinese barbecue sauce made from soybeans, vinegar, sugar, chili and seasonings. Sold in cans and in bottles. Keeps well if refrigerated once opened.

Japanese pickled ginger, or *gari,* is thinly sliced, young ginger that has been pickled in sweet vinegar. Served with sushi and sashimi. Pickled older ginger (*beni shoga*), usually less sweet, is also available in jars or plastic packets from Asian food stores.

Kaffir lime leaves have an unusual double green leaf on one stem with a very intense citrus flavor. Although available fresh, frozen or dried, nothing equals its unique and strong flavor when fresh. Use whole to infuse flavor, discarding before serving, or remove the hard stems and finely cut into very thin threads with scissors before use. Keep refrigerated. The juice and grated rind of the fruit are also used, but regular lime juice and rind can be substituted.

Nori is paper-thin sheets of dried seaweed, generally used for wrapping sushi and rice balls or thinly sliced as a garnish. Lightly toast before use or buy already toasted nori, known as yaki-nori, for a crisp texture. Must be kept airtight.

Palm sugar is a dense, heavy sugar made from different varieties of palm fruit. Available from Asian food stores in different shapes, sizes and colors it has a rich caramel flavor. Shave sugar off with a sharp knife. Avoid jars because the sugar becomes difficult to remove as it dries out. Dark brown sugar or maple sugar may be substituted.

Rice vinegar is one of the mildest vinegars available. Cider vinegar can be substituted but dilute with water as it's too strong. Rice vinegar from Japan or China is available in Asian stores.

Saffron is originally from India and is known as the queen of spices. It is picked with near religious fervor before dawn, which explains its price. Be careful not to buy counterfeits which are sometimes made with silk from corn husks and a little oil. Saffron is always used in festive dishes. You can substitute ground turmeric though it has neither the sublety nor the strength.

Sesame oil is an amber-colored aromatic oil made from toasted sesame seeds. Used to add a nutty flavor to dishes at the end of cooking. Use sparingly as it is strong. Store in a cool, dark cupboard.

Shaoxing rice wine is a Chinese rice wine that is aged for at least 10 years. Can be substituted with dry sherry or sake. Available from Asian food stores.

Sichuan peppercorns, also known as Chinese pepper or flower pepper (*hua jiao*), have a sharp pungency that tingles and slightly numbs the lips and tongue, an effect known in Chinese as ma la "numb hot". To obtain **ground Sichuan pepper**, simply dry-roast Sichuan peppercorns in a dry pan, then grind to a fine powder.

Soy sauce is a salty sauce made from fermented soybeans and wheat. Sold in bottles. Available in light and dark varieties; the dark is usually used in cooking and the lighter soy as a dipping sauce.

Sweet chili sauce is a commercial blend of a mild chili sauce with a sweet after taste. Usually used as a dipping sauce, it can also be used on burgers and barbecued meats. Store in the refrigerator after opening.

Tamarind pulp is the soft, dried pulp of the tamarind fruit that tastes like sour prunes. Although available in powdered and liquid concentrate form, the dried pulp has better flavor. Soak the required amount in boiling water for 10 minutes, breaking it up with your fingers, then drain and discard the pulp. Used in curries, marinades and soups. Available from Asian food stores. Keep airtight and refrigerate once open. Substitute very tart fruit jam or plum sauce.

Tempeh is a type of fermented soybean cake with a nutty flavor. It can be marinated before use for added flavor. It is a good meat substitute for vegetarian dishes. Available from Asian food stores.

Thick coconut cream is thick, rich liquid squeezed from shredded coconut that has been soaked in water. Available in cans or packets from most stores. Keep refrigerated once open and use within 3–4 days, or freeze. Thin coconut cream is also known as **coconut milk**. This is extracted from shredded coconut soaked in water for a second time after coconut cream is extracted. Keep refrigerated or freeze, as with coconut cream. Lite coconut milk, with lower fat content, is also available in Asian food stores.

Turmeric is a root related to ginger, with a slightly bitter, pungent flavor and intense yellow-orange color. Used to add flavor and color to dishes. Available fresh and dried from stores. Refrigerate if fresh.

Udon noodles are thick wheat noodles. They are available fresh (ready to use) or dried from Asian food stores.

Wasabi is a very hot, lime-green Japanese horseradish that is available as a paste in a tube, which should be refrigerated once opened, or as a powder that is mixed with cold water to desired consistency. Substitute hot English or Chinese mustard.

Wonton wrappers are small pliable square or round sheets of dough made from flour, egg and salt, available in various thickness. Used to wrap savory and sweet fillings. Available refrigerated or frozen. Use refrigerated wrappers within 7 days of purchase.

Appetizers

Steaming starters and appetizers makes good sense. Think ahead and make ahead, then simply refrigerate until serving—pâtés, terrines, dips, savory mousses, marinated steamed vegetables, or vegetable salads.

If you are serving hot food, many dishes can be prepared ahead and reheated in a covered steamer over boiling water when needed. You can also double-stack steamers and cook a starter with another course. Soups, stuffed vegetables, savory soufflés, dumplings, crêpe and rice paper parcels, and seafood make delectable steamed starters.

Dim sum, a steamed or deep-fried Chinese snack, is traditionally eaten between meals or for lunch. The sweet and savory dumplings, wontons, steamed buns and parcels wrapped in egg or bean curd sheets are often served in the bamboo steamers they were cooked in. For a nice serving effect, invest in a few small bamboo steamers—one per person—for individual servings. If you are double-stacking steamers remember to rotate food on the two levels to cook evenly. Wrappers are interchangeable in most recipes (see list of wrappers on page 10). Substitute wonton or pot sticker (*gow gee*) wrappers for blanched cabbage or spinach leaves, or use bean curd sheets or rice paper wrappers.

In this chapter, I have included some wonderful ideas for meal appetizers, many of which can also be used as finger foods when entertaining. Recipes such as the mouth-watering Chinese Chicken Dumplings and Five Spice Ginger Pork Rolls have a distinctly Asian flavor and showcase the lightness, texture and flavorsome results you can achieve with steaming. You can interchange the chicken for shrimp, or the ginger for chili peppers. The ingredients are easily found and the wrappers make these starters beautiful to serve.

The Barbecued Pork Rice Nibbles and the Chicken Balls on Rosemary Sprigs are two other delicious examples of how to present food in a creative, yet simple way.

The varieties and possibilities are endless. Try expanding on the ideas within this book and interchanging ingredients. Your imagination is the only limit!

Steamed Mussels with Garlic Herb Butter
(see recipe on page 22)

Chinese Chicken Dumplings

Everyone love dumplings—witness their appearance in one form or another in cuisines around the world. These delicious chicken dumplings are inspired by the Cantonese style Chinese dumplings that are standard fare in dim sum. As an alternative to chicken, try minced shrimp, scallop, tofu or crunchy vegetables.

8 oz (250 g) ground chicken
4 green onions (scallions), finely chopped
$1/4$ clove garlic, crushed
$1/4$ cup (45 g) roasted peanuts, finely chopped
$1/4$ cup (10 g) fresh coriander leaves
   (cilantro), chopped
1 tablespoon bottled sweet chili sauce
2 teaspoons soy sauce
$1/2$ teaspoon fish sauce
16 round wonton wrappers

Chili Sauce
$1/4$ cup (60 ml) rice vinegar
$1/4$ cup (60 ml) fresh lime juice
2 teaspoons fish sauce
1 tablespoon shaved palm sugar or dark
   brown sugar
1 tablespoon water
1 clove garlic, crushed
1 finger-length red chili pepper, deseeded
   and finely chopped

Note: To make flower dumplings (see photo on page 4) instead of flat dumplings, fill the wrapper, gather the edges around the filling, forming a basket. Gently squeeze the center of the dumpling to expose the filling at the top. Tap bottom of dumpling on a clean work surface to flatten.

Makes 16 dumplings

1 In a bowl, combine the chicken, green onions, garlic, peanuts, coriander leaves, chili sauce, soy sauce and fish sauce. Place the wrappers on a clean work surface and cover with a damp kitchen towel. Take one wrapper and place in a *gow gee* press or on a clean work surface. Spoon 2 teaspoons of filling onto center of wrapper. Brush the edges of wrapper with water, close seal of press, or fold in half, pressing with fingers to seal and make a frilled edge. Cover with a damp kitchen towel and repeat with the remaining wrappers and filling.
2 Combine all the Chili Sauce ingredients in a bowl, stirring constantly until the sugar dissolves.
3 Place the dumplings in a steamer or steamer basket lined with parchment (baking) paper, leaving some space for steam to circulate efficiently. Partially fill a wok or pot with water (steamer or basket should not touch the water) and bring to a rapid boil. Place the steamer over the boiling water and cover. Steam for 10 minutes. Serve the dumplings warm with the Chili Sauce on the side.

Barbecued Pork Rice Nibbles

This elegant show-stopper of an appetizer—perfect for entertaining—requires just a few steps to assemble. The bright flavors of citrus, fresh coriander and ginger are softened with creamy coconut milk, creating a delicious balance of flavors.

$1^1/_2$ tablespoons tamarind pulp

$^1/_2$ cup (125 ml) boiling water

1 cup (220 g) uncooked white glutinous rice

2 teaspoons grated fresh turmeric

1 teaspoon grated fresh ginger

$^3/_4$ cup (180 ml) coconut milk

2 green onions (scallions), finely chopped

$^1/_4$ cup (10 g) fresh coriander leaves (cilantro), finely chopped

3 kaffir lime leaves, spines removed, finely chopped (optional)

$^1/_4$ teaspoon grated kaffir lime rind

1 finger-length red chili pepper, deseeded and finely chopped (optional)

6 oz (185 g) barbecued pork (available from Asian food stores) or barbecued chicken, sliced

Sweet chili, barbecue or hoisin sauce, for serving

Makes 16–20 squares

1 Place the tamarind pulp in a small bowl and cover with the boiling water. Mix well, breaking up the pulp with a spoon to release the flavor. Let stand for 5 minutes, then push through a fine-meshed strainer, discarding the pulp and reserving the liquid.
2 Wrap the turmeric in a cheesecloth (muslin) square and tie with string. Put the rice, turmeric and tamarind liquid in a medium bowl. Cover with cold water and let soak overnight. Drain, removing the turmeric. Line a bamboo steamer or steamer basket with cheese-cloth (muslin) and spread the rice evenly on top.
3 Partially fill a wok or pot with water (steamer should not touch the water) and bring to a rapid boil. Place the steamer over the water, cover and steam until the rice is just tender, 30–35 minutes, adding more water to the wok if required. Remove steamer from the heat and put the rice in a bowl.
4 Gently fold in the grated ginger, coconut cream, green onions, coriander leaves, kaffir lime leaves and rind, and chili pepper. Spread the rice evenly in an 8-inch (20-cm) square baking pan lined with parchment (baking) paper and refrigerate until set, about 2 hours. Cut into 16–20 squares to serve. Top with a small piece of barbecued pork or chicken and a dash of sweet chili, satay or hoisin sauce.

Note: If you have difficulty finding preprepared barbecued pork or chicken, an easy solution is to buy a rotisserie chicken from your supermarket. Shred 6 oz (185 g) of light and dark chicken meat into small pieces and lightly coat with home-made or bottled barbecue sauce of your choice. Let rest in the refrigerator for an hour or more before using.

Five Spice Ginger Pork Rolls

This classic Asian appetizer is usually fried. In this delicious low-fat version, minced pork is combined with thinly sliced vegetables and signature seasonings—such as fresh ginger, five spice powder and aromatic toasted sesame oil—for a delicious result.

8 oz (250 g) ground pork

3 green onions (scallions), finely chopped

2 tablespoons chopped canned bamboo shoots or water chestnuts

1 teaspoon grated fresh ginger

$1/4$ teaspoon five spice powder

2 teaspoons soy sauce

1 teaspoon sesame oil

8 dried bean curd skin wrappers, 5 by 6 inches (13 by 15 cm)

$1/4$ small red bell pepper, deseeded and thinly sliced

4 green onions (scallions), green tops only, cut into 5-inch (13-cm) lengths

Hoisin and Ginger Dipping Sauce

$1/4$ cup (60 ml) hoisin sauce

2 tablespoons Shaoxing rice wine or dry sherry

2 teaspoons chopped fresh ginger

1 clove garlic, crushed

1 green onion (scallion), finely chopped

Note: If you cannot find dried bean curd skins, then use cabbage leaves instead. Lightly steam 8 cabbage leaves to soften them, then drain well and use in place of the bean curd skin wrappers.

Makes 8 rolls

1 Place the pork, green onions, bamboo shoots, grated ginger, five spice powder, soy sauce and sesame oil in a bowl and mix until well combined. Lightly brush the dried bean curd skins with cold water to soften them, and lay flat on a clean work surface. Spread $1/8$ of the pork mixture along one end of each sheet. Lay the strips of red bell pepper and green onions along the pork mixture and push gently until completely enclosed by the mixture. Fold the two sides of the sheet in and roll up, brushing the remaining side lightly with water if needed. Press down firmly to seal.

2 Partially fill a large wok or pot with water (steamer should not touch the water) and bring to a rapid boil. Line a bamboo steamer or steamer basket with parchment (baking) paper or leaves, leaving some space for steam to circulate efficiently. Arrange the rolls in a single layer in the steamer. Place the steamer over the water, cover, and cook until the pork mixture is firm and ready, about 10 minutes.

3 Combine all the Hoisin and Ginger Dipping Sauce ingredients in a bowl and mix well.

4 Remove the rolls from the steamer. Serve with the Hoisin and Ginger Dipping Sauce on the side.

Steamed Mussels with Garlic Herb Butter

Steamed mussels is one the quickest and easiest dinners I know of, and this flavorful recipe won't disappoint.

2 lbs (1 kg) fresh mussels
$1/_2$ cup (1 stick/125 g) softened butter
2 cloves garlic, crushed
2 tablespoons chopped fresh parsley
2 tablespoons chopped fresh chives
1 teaspoon grated lime rind
Freshly cracked black pepper to taste

Note: You can substitute Basil Pesto (page 59) for the butter mixture, and this recipe also works well with fresh shelled and deveined shrimp.

1 Scrub the mussels under cold running water with a nylon pad or stiff brush and pull off hair-like "beards," discarding any mussels that are cracked or do not close when tapped. Place them in a large bamboo steamer or steamer basket.
2 Mix the butter with the rest of the ingredients in a small bowl.
3 Partially fill a large wok or pot with water (steamer should not touch the water) and bring to a rapid boil. Place the steamer over the water, cover and steam until the mussels open, 4–6 minutes. Remove from the steamer, spoon the butter mixture into each shell, and serve immediately with a tossed green salad and crusty bread.

Serves 4

Chicken Balls on Rosemary Sprigs

Your guests will love the delicate flavor—accented with fresh herbs and yogurt—of this whimsical appetizer.

8 rosemary sprigs, about 5 inches (13 cm) long

12 oz (350 g) ground chicken

1 small onion, finely diced

2 cloves garlic, crushed

2 tablespoons plain yogurt

1 teaspoon ground cumin

1 tablespoon chopped fresh coriander
  leaves (cilantro)

1 tablespoon chopped fresh mint leaves

2 teaspoons cornstarch

Salt and freshly ground black pepper

1 Cut each rosemary sprig in half, stripping off all the leaves except for a tuft at one end. Wash and pat dry with paper towels. Place the chicken, onion, garlic, yogurt, cumin, coriander and mint leaves, cornstarch, salt, and pepper in a bowl and mix until well combined. With damp hands, shape about 1 tablespoon of the mixture firmly around each rosemary sprig. Place in a steamer on individual pieces of parchment (baking) paper.

2 Partially fill a wok or pot with water and bring to a rapid boil. Place the steamer over the boiling water, cover and steam until the chicken is cooked, about 10 minutes.

Makes 16 balls

Stuffed Zucchini Slices

These beautiful and refreshingly light zucchini rounds can easily be made as a vegetarian or vegan option by simply substituting tofu for the chicken and vegetable stock for the chicken stock.

2 dried black Chinese mushrooms
1 large zucchini (about $1^1/_4$ lbs/625 g)
8 oz (250 g) ground chicken
2 green onions (scallions), finely chopped
1 clove garlic, minced
1 tablespoon soy sauce
1 teaspoon Shaoxing rice wine or dry sherry
$^1/_2$ teaspoon sesame oil
1 teaspoon grated fresh ginger

Sauce
$^1/_2$ cup (125 ml) chicken stock
2 tablespoons oyster sauce
1 finger-length red chili pepper, deseeded and finely chopped (optional)
3 teaspoons cornstarch
1 teaspoon water

Serves 4 as a starter or light lunch with salad

1 Soak the mushrooms in hot water for 15 minutes. Drain, gently squeezing out excess water. Discard the stems and finely chop the caps.
2 Cut the zucchini into 1-inch (2.5-cm) slices. Scoop out the seeds with a teaspoon. Combine the mushrooms, chicken, green onions, garlic, soy sauce, wine or sherry, sesame oil and ginger in a bowl, mixing well. Spoon approximately 2 tablespoons chicken mixture into the center of each zucchini slice, molding the mixture $^1/_2$ inch (12 mm) above the slice. Place the slices on individual pieces of parchment (baking) paper, and place them in a 12-inch (30-cm) bamboo steamer or steamer basket. (If using a two-level steamer, switch levels halfway through for even cooking.)
3 Partially fill a wok or pot with water (steamer should not touch the water) and bring to a rapid boil. Place the steamer over the water, cover and steam until the melon is tender, 10–15 minutes.
4 Make the Sauce by heating the stock, oyster sauce and chili pepper in a small saucepan. Mix the cornstarch and water, then stir in 1 tablespoon hot stock. Add to the remaining stock, stirring constantly until thickened.
5 Serve the zucchini slices with the Sauce poured over on a bed of Garlic Mashed Potatoes (page 41).

Chicken and Spinach Wontons

These bite-size dumplings—a Chinese specialty indispensible in the famous wonton soup—make a great prelude to any meal or a wonderful party snack. A sweet, spicy chili sauce adds some excitement to these otherwise mild dumplings.

1 bunch spinach, stems removed, leaves washed
8 oz (250 g) ground chicken
3 green onions (scallions), finely chopped
1 teaspoon grated fresh ginger
2 cloves garlic, crushed
2 teaspoons soy sauce
1 teaspoon sesame oil
$1/2$ teaspoon fish sauce
1 finger-length red chili pepper, deseeded and finely chopped (optional)
3 teaspoons cornstarch
30 wonton wrappers

Sweet Chili Sauce
$1/4$ cup (60 ml) rice vinegar
2 tablespoons sugar
2 tablespoons water
1 teaspoon lemon juice
$3/4$ teaspoon fish sauce
1 finger-length red chili pepper, finely chopped (seeds removed for milder taste)

1 Place the spinach in a bamboo steamer or steamer basket. Partially fill a wok or pot with water (steamer should not touch the water), and bring to a rapid boil. Put steamer over the water, cover and steam until the spinach is soft, 2–3 minutes. Remove from the heat and let cool. Squeeze out the excess water and chop finely.
2 Put the spinach in a medium bowl and add the chicken, green onions, ginger, garlic, soy sauce, sesame oil, fish sauce, chili pepper and cornstarch, mixing well.
3 Place wonton wrappers on a clean work surface and cover with a damp kitchen towel. Working with 1 wrapper at a time, place 2 teaspoons of the filling onto the center of a wrapper. Brush the edges of the wrapper with water. Gather the edges together and twist to seal or fold the wrapper in half and press the edges together with your fingers to seal. Cover with a damp kitchen towel and set aside. Repeat with the remaining wrappers.
4 Combine all the Sweet Chili Sauce ingredients in a bowl, stirring well until the sugar dissolves.
5 Line a large bamboo steamer or steamer basket with parchment (baking) paper. Partially fill a large wok or pot with water (steamer should not touch the water) and bring to a rapid boil. Arrange the dumplings in the steamer, making sure they do not touch. Place the steamer over the water, cover and steam for 10 minutes, adding more water to the pot as necessary. Remove the steamer from the wok or pot and carefully remove the dumplings. Serve warm, with the Sweet Chili Sauce on the side.

Makes 30

Vegetables

Steaming is one of the best methods for cooking vegetables. The method is the same for most vegetables; only the time varies. Put washed vegetables in a bamboo steamer or steamer basket. Partially fill a wok or pot with water (steaming surface should not touch the water) and bring to a rapid boil. Place the steamer over the water, cover and steam until the vegetables are cooked. Line bamboo steamers with cheesecloth (muslin) or parchment (baking) paper if small vegetables could fall through the bamboo slats.

Make a selection of vegetables with similar cooking times, cut them into similar-sized pieces, and steam until just tender. Toss with butter, olive oil, lemon juice, balsamic vinegar or soy sauce. Garnish with toasted sesame seeds, chopped fresh herbs, toasted bread crumbs, sliced green onions or toasted nuts.

Guide for Steaming Times

2–4 minutes: Asian greens such as bok choy, Shanghai bok choy, choy sum (2–3 minutes or until leaves are wilted); Chinese broccoli (*gai lan*; 3–4 minutes or until stems are tender); Chinese cabbage and spinach; mushrooms; snow peas; sliced zucchini

4–8 minutes: Asparagus; fava (broad) beans, sugar snap peas, peas; broccoli and cauliflower florets; carrots and parsnips, sliced; potatoes and sweet potatoes, diced or sliced; cabbage and swiss chard (silverbeet); corn on the cob; brussels sprouts

8–15 minutes: Potatoes and sweet potatoes, overlapped slices, 10–15 minutes; baby new potatoes, 12–18 minutes; celery root (celeriac), diced

15 minutes or more: Eggplant (aubergine), whole or half; potatoes, whole; beets (beetroots), whole (15–20 minutes if small, 35–45 minutes if large)

Garlic Mashed Potatoes (see recipe on page 41)

Marinated Corn on the Cob

Marinated corn on the cob is an inventive way to add some excitement to this classic summertime fare. Try one of these marinades to give fresh corn on the cob a different flavor sensation that's sure to surprise your family and friends.

4 fresh ears corn, husks removed

Marinade No. 1
1 tablespoon soy sauce
1 tablespoon olive oil
$1/2$ teaspoon sesame oil
1 clove garlic, crushed

Marinade No. 2
1 tablespoon sweet bottled chili sauce
1 teaspoon fish sauce
$1/2$ teaspoon sesame oil
1 clove garlic, crushed
1 teaspoon grated lemon or Sichuan pepper
2 tablespoons chopped fresh coriander
  leaves (cilantro)

Combine the Marinade ingredients in a shallow dish and pour it over the corn. Refrigerate for several hours or overnight, turning the corn occasionally. Wrap each cob in parchment (baking) paper, twisting the ends to seal. Cook in a covered steamer over rapidly boiling water until tender, 6–8 minutes.

Serves 4

Potatoes with Lemon Dill Butter

Lemon rind adds finesse to this steamed take on boiled new potatoes—the classic side dish that has adorned many a Sunday potroast or meatloaf. New potatoes are simply young potatoes (any type) that have tender thin skins, which saves you the task of peeling them, making this dish quick and easy to prepare.

$1^1/_2$ lbs (700 g) unpeeled baby potatoes, washed
1–2 tablespoons butter
1 teaspoon grated lemon rind
1–2 tablespoons chopped fresh dill or parsley
Freshly ground black pepper to taste

Serves 4–6

Put potatoes in a bamboo steamer or steamer basket. Partially fill a wok or pot with water (steamer should not touch the water) and bring to a rapid boil. Put steamer over the water, cover and steam until the potatoes are tender, 12–18 minutes, depending on size. (Potatoes are done when easily pierced with a skewer.) Toss the potatoes with the butter, lemon rind and dill or parsley. Sprinkle with pepper.

Green Beans with Toasted Macadamia Nuts

The buttery-rich and slightly sweet flavor of macadamia nuts makes these garlicky green beans hard to resist. Be sure to store left-over macadamia nuts in the refrigerator to prolong freshness. Their high fat content will cause the nuts to turn rancid if stored at room temperature.

12 oz (350 g) green beans, trimmed
Freshly ground black pepper to taste
1–2 tablespoons butter
$^1/_2$ cup (75 g) toasted macadamia nuts, coarsely chopped
2 cloves garlic, crushed

Serves 4

1 Put the beans in a bamboo steamer or steamer basket. Partially fill a wok or pot with water (steamer should not touch the water) and bring to a rapid boil. Put the steamer over the water, cover and steam until the beans are cooked but still firm, 4–5 minutes. Transfer the beans to a bowl and sprinkle with pepper.
2 While the beans are cooking, melt the butter in a small saucepan, add the nuts and garlic, and brown lightly. Remove from the heat and pour over the beans.

Baby Beet Salad with Mint Orange Dressing

With its beet-red and bright orange colors, this refreshing mint and citrus-flavored salad is as delicious as it is beautiful. For extra visual excitement, try a range of different colored beets—from white to yellow to the striped Chioggia beet, known as the "candy cane" variety.

2 bunches baby beets, washed and trimmed
2 oranges, peeled and segmented
1 red onion, thinly sliced
3 cups (90 g) mixed salad greens
$^1/_4$ cup (50 g) almonds, toasted and
  coarsely chopped, for garnish

Mint Orange Dressing
$^1/_2$ cup (125 ml) freshly squeezed orange
  juice
$^1/_4$ cup (60 ml) olive oil
$^1/_4$ cup (60 ml) rice vinegar
1 tablespoon chopped fresh mint leaves
Salt and freshly ground pepper to taste

Serves 4–6

1 Make the Mint Orange Dressing by combining all the ingredients in a bowl. Mix until well combined.
2 Place the beets in a bamboo steamer or steamer basket. Partially fill a wok or pot with water (steamer should not touch the water) and bring to a rapid boil. Place the steamer over the water, cover and steam until the beets are tender, 15–20 minutes (35–45 minutes for medium size). Test by inserting a skewer into the thickest part. Immerse in cold water until cool enough to handle, then drain. Gently peel off the skin, and halve or slice beets depending on size. While still warm, toss with the Dressing, then refrigerate for 1 hour. Drain the beets, reserving the Dressing.
3 Arrange the beets, orange segments and onion slices on the salad greens. Pour the Mint Orange Dressing over the salad, and garnish with the toasted almonds.

Note: Toast the almonds by placing them in a frying pan over medium heat, and fry until lightly browned, stirring constantly, for 3–4 minutes. Be careful not to burn.

Asparagus Spears with Garlic Mayonnaise Dip

Nothing says spring better than fresh asparagus, and it is particularly enjoyable with this delicious mayonnaise dip.

2 bunches fresh asparagus
2–3 cups (60–90 g) baby spinach leaves or
   baby arugula (rocket)
2 green onions (scallions), green part only,
   thinly sliced, for garnish

Garlic Mayonnaise Dip
2 egg yolks
$2^1/_2$ tablespoons fresh lemon juice
Pinch of salt and freshly ground black pepper
$^3/_4$ cup (180 ml) olive oil
2 teaspoons crushed garlic, or to taste

Serves 4–6

1 Wash the asparagus and trim off the woody base. (Young, thin asparagus should snap when bent where woodiness begins. Peel lower part of thick asparagus with a knife or vegetable peeler.)
2 Place asparagus in a bamboo steamer or steamer basket and steam until the asparagus is tender but still crisp, 5–10 minutes depending on thickness. Immediately drop them into cold water to stop cooking. Arrange asparagus on the arugula leaves.
3 Make the Garlic Mayonnaise by combining the egg yolks, lemon juice, salt and pepper in a blender and process until smooth. With machine running, gradually add the olive oil in a thin stream, slowly at first until the mixture begins to thicken, then faster. Stir in the garlic, mixing well until no lumps remain.
4 Serve as an appetizer or salad, with Garlic Mayonnaise drizzled over and garnished with green onions.

Stuffed Zucchini Blossoms

Zucchini blossoms—a delicate springtime treat—are available at farmers' markets and better grocery stores.

2 green onions (scallions), finely sliced
1 clove garlic, finely chopped
1 cup (150 g) cooked rice
3 tablespoons grated Parmesan
2 tablespoons chopped fresh parsley
2 tablespoons chopped fresh dill
1 small tomato, deseeded
2 teaspoons capers
Salt and freshly ground pepper to taste
2 eggs, separated
12–16 zucchini (courgette) blossoms
Balsamic or red wine vinegar for sprinkling

1 Mix the green onions, garlic, rice, cheese, parsley, dill, tomato, capers, salt and pepper in a bowl. In another bowl, lightly beat the egg yolks, then stir into the rice mixture. In a large bowl, beat the egg whites until soft peaks form. Gently fold into the rice mixture. Hold the zucchini blossoms open and fill each one three-fourths full with the rice mixture, folding the petals over to hold the mixture in.
2 Line a 12-inch (30-cm) bamboo steamer with parchment (baking) paper or banana leaves, and carefully place the zucchini blossoms in a circle. Cover and steam until cooked, 6–8 minutes. (Zucchini is done when easily pierced with a skewer.) Serve hot or at room temperature as an appetizer, with a sprinkling of balsamic vinegar.

Makes 12–16 (allow 2–3 per person depending on size)

Tasty Squash Soup with Hazelnuts

This wholesome soup makes a great lunch on a crisp fall or winter day. Yet with a touch of fresh ginger and an elegant garnish of fresh herbs, chopped nuts and yogurt, this versatile soup is perfect for an elegant dinner.

4 butternut squash or baby pumpkins,
  3¹/₂ lbs (1.8 kg) total
1 tablespoon oil
2 cloves garlic, crushed
1 small yellow onion, chopped
1 teaspoon grated fresh ginger
4 cups (1 liter) chicken or vegetable stock
Salt and pepper to taste
4 teaspoons plain yogurt or sour cream
12 sprigs watercress
¹/₂ cup (75 g) hazelnuts, toasted, skinned
  and coarsely chopped (see note)

Serves 4

1 Partially fill a large wok or pot with water (steamer or basket should not touch the water) and bring to a rapid boil. Place whole squash in the oiled steamer. Place the steamer over the water, cover, and steam until the squash are just tender, 40–45 minutes. Remove steamer from the wok before removing the squash.
2 Place the squash on a board, flatter side down (take care, as it will be hot). Cut the tops off and discard. Discard the seeds, and scoop out the flesh to within ¹/₄ inch (6 mm) of skin, being careful not to break through. Turn the squash upside down to drain, adding any drained juice to the flesh. Purée the squash flesh. Cover the shells with foil to keep warm.
3 Heat the oil in a medium saucepan over medium heat. Fry the garlic, onion and ginger until softened but not brown, 4–5 minutes. Add the puréed squash, stock, salt and pepper and simmer for 10 minutes. Pour the soup into the shells and serve garnished with yogurt, watercress and hazelnuts.

Note: Toast the hazelnuts in a preheated oven 350°F (180°C) for 8–10 minutes. Fold in a kitchen towel and rub together to remove skins. Squash and soup can be prepared the day before serving and chilled. If reheating soup in a saucepan, steam the squash for 10–15 minutes to heat through before filling with hot soup. To reheat soup in shells by steaming, allow 45 minutes.
For variation, omit hazelnuts and add 8 medium shrimp, peeled, deveined and chopped with some garlic and green onions. Cover and steam until cooked and soup is bright orange, 3–4 minutes.

Garlic Mashed Potatoes

Why eat humdrum mashed potatoes when you can enjoy the pleasures of Garlic Mashed Potatoes—one of the most versatile and all-time favorite sides invented. Garlic Mashed Potatoes go equally well with poultry, meat or fish.

4 unpeeled cloves garlic

3–4 large potatoes (1¼ lbs/600 g), peeled and diced

½–¾ cup (125–180 ml) milk, heated

2 tablespoons butter, softened

1–2 tablespoons chopped fresh chives

Salt and freshly ground black pepper to taste

1 tablespoon heavy (double) cream (optional)

Serves 4

1 Place the garlic in a frying pan over medium-low heat. Cook until the cloves are soft and skins are lightly browned, 10–12 minutes, moving pan occasionally to prevent garlic burning. Leave until cool to touch. Squeeze garlic out of their skins and mash with a fork.

2 Place potatoes in bottom level of a bamboo steamer or a steamer basket lined with cheesecloth (muslin), and cover. Partially fill a wok or pot with water (steamer should not touch the water) and bring to a rapid boil. Put steamer over the water, cover and steam until the potatoes are tender, 6–8 minutes. Heat the milk in a small saucepan or a microwave or, if using a two-level bamboo steamer, put the milk in a heatproof bowl, cover with plastic wrap, and place on level above the potatoes to heat through.

3 Remove the potatoes from the steamer, place in a bowl, and mash with a whisk or fork. Gradually stir in the butter, chives, garlic, salt and pepper, then add enough hot milk and cream, if desired, for a creamy consistency. Keep warm by covering with plastic wrap and placing in the covered steamer over simmering water until needed.

Steamed Asian Greens with Oyster Sauce

Quick-cooking greens and mushrooms are perfectly suited to steaming, which brings out all their flavor without losing nutrition. The richness of oyster sauce adds depth to this satisfying side dish. To make this a vegetarian dish, substitute mushroom sauce or 2 tablespoons of soy sauce in place of the oyster sauce.

1 bunch bok choy or choy sum, trimmed
  and cut into lengths
1 cake (5 oz/150 g) tempeh or firm tofu, cut
  into $1/2$-inch (12-mm) pieces
1 small bunch (3 oz/90 g) enoki mushrooms, trimmed
1 cup (100 g) canned baby corn, halved
$1/4$ cup (60 ml) oyster sauce
1 clove garlic, crushed
1 teaspoon sesame oil
$1/2$ teaspoon grated fresh ginger
2 green onions (scallions), finely chopped
1 tablespoon toasted sesame seeds (see note)

Note: Toast the sesame seeds in a frying pan over medium heat until golden brown. Keep moving the pan so the seeds do not burn. For variation, add steamed peeled fresh shrimp (3–5 minutes) or scallops (2–3 minutes), and toss with the bok choy just before serving. To turn this into a delightful noodle dish, blanch 8 oz (250 g) fresh udon or egg noodles in hot water for 2–3 minutes while the vegetables are steaming. Serve the noodles with the vegetables spooned on top.

1 Put the bok choy, tempeh or tofu, enoki and baby corn in a large bamboo steamer or steamer basket. Partially fill a wok or pot with water (steamer should not touch the water) and bring to a rapid boil. Place the steamer over the water, cover and steam until the vegetables are softened, 3–4 minutes.
2 Meanwhile, put the oyster sauce, garlic, sesame oil and ginger in a small saucepan and mix well. Place the saucepan over medium heat to warm the sauce, 3–4 minutes.
3 Remove vegetables from the steamer and arrange on serving plates with the enoki in the center. Drizzle the warm sauce over the vegetables. Sprinkle with green onions and sesame seeds. Serve as a side dish or light vegetarian dish, or with noodles as a main course (see Note).

Serves 2–4

Rice and Grains

Most grains and legumes steam well, although some require soaking before cooking, which softens them and reduces the cooking time. Always leave rice in a covered steamer for 5–10 minutes after cooking to allow all moisture to be completely absorbed and soggy patches to disappear. If a softer rice is preferred, let cooked rice to sit a little longer.

To reheat rice: Place rice in a heatproof bowl and sit in a bamboo steamer or steamer basket. Place over rapidly simmering water, cover and steam until heated through, 10–15 minutes. Rice will become quite firm and chewy if refrigerated. In this book we have used sticky rice (another name for glutinous rice), sushi rice (made with short- or medium-grain rice) and black glutinous rice. Glutinous rice becomes sticky and sweet when cooked; black glutinous rice becomes a light purple color when cooked.

Lentils: Lentils cook very well in a steamer after soaking. Some need to be soaked longer than others. The *masoor dhal*, or red lentil, is the quickest to cook and can be eaten as a dip with raw vegetables or pita bread, or simply as an accompaniment to an Indian meal.

Couscous: These days most Westerners opt for the convenience of using instant couscous. Those without their own couscousière can simply use a bamboo steamer or steamer basket lined with cheesecloth (muslin) that fits snugly into a large wok or pot.

General Guide for Steaming Times

Rice: Steamed white rice, 20–25 minutes; steamed brown rice, 35–45 minutes; black or white glutinous rice, 40–45 minutes

Chickpeas: Soaked, steam 60 minutes

Lentils: Unsoaked, steam 40–45 minutes; soaked for 30–60 minutes, steam 25–30 minutes

Couscous: Soaked for 10 minutes, steam 30 minutes

Instant couscous: Soaked for 4–5 minutes, steam 10–15 minutes

Noodles (cooked, not steamed): Fresh udon and egg noodles, 2–3 minutes; dried egg noodles, 5 minutes; dried udon noodles, 6–10 minutes (different sizes available); dried Italian pasta, 8–10 minutes

Perfect Steamed Rice in a Steamer

Rice is the cornerstone to numerous cuisines around the world, and it goes with several recipes in this book. Using this recipe, you'll find it's easy to make perfect rice everytime. For flavored rice, cook rice with a small pinch of saffron threads, a pinch of ground saffron or ground turmeric, or add a little grated ginger.

1 cup (220 g) uncooked long-grain white rice
$1^1/_4$ cups (310 ml) cold water or stock

Serves 2–3

Note: For variation, cook rice with a small pinch of saffron threads, a pinch of ground saffron, or ground turmeric, or add a little grated ginger.

Put the rice in a fine-meshed sieve and rinse under cold running water. Let drain for 5 minutes, then place in a heatproof bowl that fits in the steamer. Add the water. Fill a wok or pot with water (water should not touch the steamer) and bring to a rapid boil. Place the steamer over the water, cover and steam the rice until tender and the water has evaporated, 20–25 minutes. Remove pot or wok from the heat. Place a cloth under the lid to stop any condensation from dripping back onto the rice, and let stand for 5–10 minutes. Fluff rice with a fork and serve. If not using rice immediately, refrigerate, and reheat when needed.

Perfect Steamed Rice in a Pot

This easy technique will allow you to steam a full meal with rice in one go—a great method for getting weekday dinners to the table quickly.

In liquid in pot, with meat or vegetables steaming above

2 cups (500 ml) cold water or stock
1 cup (220 g) uncooked long-grain white rice

Serves 2–3

Bring the water to a boil in a pot. Add the rice, stirring well, and return to a boil. Place a bamboo steamer or steamer basket with meat or vegetables inside over the water, cover and steam until the liquid is absorbed, 12–15 minutes. Remove from the heat and stand, covered, for 5–10 minutes. Fluff with a fork and serve. If not using immediately, refrigerate rice and reheat when needed.

Note: If cooking more than 1 cup long-grain rice, only add $1^1/_2$ cups (375 ml) liquid per cup rice after the first cup.
Herbed rice: For variation, cook 1 cup (220 g) long-grain rice according to one of the above recipes. Gently fold in $^1/_3$ cup (15 g) finely chopped fresh herbs such as parsley or coriander leaves (cilantro).

Sushi Rice

Sushi rice is made with ordinary short- or medium-grain rice. What makes it special is the slightly sweet-and-salty vinegar sauce that is used to flavor the rice, give it a glossy appearance and make it extra sticky—thus allowing it to perform its job as a base for other ingredients, most famously raw fish and seafood.

1½ cups (300 g) uncooked short- or
  medium-grain rice
1½ cups (375 ml) cold water

Sushi Vinegar
¼ cup (60 ml) rice vinegar
2 tablespoons sugar
¼ teaspoon salt

Makes about 4½ cups (675 g)

1 Wash rice in 3 or 4 changes of cold water until the water is clear. Let drain for 5 minutes, then place in a bowl that fits in a bamboo steamer or steamer basket, and add the water. Let soak for 30 minutes. Place in the steamer. Partially fill a wok or pot with water (steamer should not touch the water) and bring to a rapid boil. Place the steamer over the water, cover and steam until the rice is cooked and the water evaporated, 20–25 minutes. Remove from the heat and let stand for 10 minutes with a cloth under the lid to stop any condensation from dripping back onto the rice. If softer rice is preferred, let rice stand slightly longer.
2 Make the Sushi Vinegar by combining all the ingredients in a small bowl, stirring until the sugar and salt dissolve completely. The mixture can be heated over low heat if required. (Sushi Vinegar ingredients can be altered according to taste.)
3 Put the hot rice in a flat, shallow, non-metallic dish and pour the Sushi Vinegar over. With a wooden paddle or spoon, slice through the rice at a 45-degree angle to break up any lumps and distribute the Vinegar evenly. Fan cool for 5–8 minutes, turning the rice 2 to 3 times for even cooling. Cover with a damp kitchen towel to stop rice from drying out until served.

California Rolls

These rolls, as their name suggests, were invented in California, although these thick-style sushi rolls originated in the Osaka area of Japan. Avocado is the special ingredient that gives these rolls a California flair.

4 cups (600 g) prepared Sushi Rice (page 49)
4 sheets nori
8 teaspoons flying fish roe or salmon roe
1 Japanese or hothouse English cucumber, cut into thin, lengthwise strips
8 jumbo shrimp or king prawns, cooked and peeled, deveined and halved lengthwise
1 ripe avocado, peeled, pitted and sliced lengthwise into thin strips

Tezu Vinegar Water
1 cup (250 ml) water
2 tablespoons rice vinegar
1 teaspoon water

Makes 4 rolls (32 pieces)

1 Prepare the Sushi Rice by following the recipe on page 49.
2 Combine the Tezu Vinegar Water ingredients in a bowl and mix well.
3 Lay 1 nori sheet lengthwise on a bamboo rolling mat, shiny side down. Wet your hands in the bowl of Tezu Vinegar Water to avoid the rice from sticking, take 1 cup (150 g) of the Sushi Rice and place it on the nori sheet.

4 Spread the rice evenly, leaving a $^3/_4$-in (2-cm) strip along the top edge uncovered. Build a low ridge of rice in front of this uncovered strip to keep filling in place.

5 Spoon 2 teaspoons of the fish roe and spread it along the center of the rice. Lay 2 shrimp pieces with several cucumber strips on top of it.

6 Top with strips of avocado placed along the center on top of the other fillings.

7 Roll the mat over once, pressing the ingredients in to keep the roll firm and leaving the exposed strip of nori at the top edge free.

8 While covering the roll (but not the open strip of nori), hold the rolling mat in position and press all around to make the roll firm. Lift up the top of the rolling mat and turn the roll over to overlap the inner edge of the nori strip to seal the roll.

9 Roll the entire roll once more, and press to shape it. Using a very sharp knife, cut each roll in half, then cut each half in half again. Then cut each quarter in half to make a total of 8 equal segments as shown on page 50.

Classic Nigiri Sushi

The most popular type of sushi served in restaurants, this simple-to-make sushi is sure to impress your guests.

2 cups (300 g) prepared Sushi Rice (page 49)
7 oz (200 g) raw fish (salmon or tuna),
  sliced into 16 strips measuring $2^1/_2$ x $1^1/_4$
  x $^1/_4$ in (6 x 3 x $^1/_2$ cm) or other toppings
  of your choice
Wasabi paste, to taste
Japanese Pickled Ginger (purchased), to serve
Soy sauce, for dipping

Tezu Vinegar Water
1 cup (250 ml) water
2 tablespoons rice vinegar
1 teaspoon salt

Note: Buy only sushi-grade fish. Before using salmon, cover it with salt and marinate for 1 hour, then rinse off the salt and place it in the freezer.

1 Prepare the Sushi Rice by following the recipe on page 49.
2 Put the Tezu Vinegar Water ingredients in a bowl and mix well.
3 To shape the rice, first moisten your hands in the bowl of Tezu to prevent the rice from sticking to your hands, then take 2 tablespoons of the Sushi Rice and shape it into an oval "finger", pressing it gently to form a small log. Pick up a slice of the topping using your left hand and dab a little wasabi (if using) on it with your right index finger.
4 Place the rice "finger" on top of the topping and press it onto the wasabi-dabbed topping with your index finger. Then turn the rice and topping over so that the topping is on top. Using your index finger and middle finger, mold the topping around the rice, pressing it gently around the rice so that the rice does not show around the edges of the topping. Repeat with the remaining ingredients to make a total of 16 sushi.
5 Arrange the sushi on a serving platter and serve immediately with mounds of wasabi paste, Japanese Pickled Ginger and small dipping bowls of soy sauce.

Makes 16 sushi

Step-by step Nigiri Sushi

1 Hold a slice of the topping with your left hand. Using the tip of your right index finger, dab a little wasabi on the topping.

2 Using your index finger, press the rice onto the wasabi-dabbed topping.

3 Turn over so that topping is on top. Use your index and middle fingers to mold and gently press topping down onto the rice.

Curried Vegetables with Pistachio Couscous

This colorful vegetable dish is flavored with the seductively aromatic ground spices and fresh herbs of North African cuisine. A sprinkling of toasted pistachios adds color and a rich and satisfying flavor accent. To make the dish vegetarian, cook the couscous in vegetable stock instead of chicken stock. This dish is also delicious served over rice instead of couscous.

1 medium eggplant, cut into small pieces
Coarse sea salt for sprinkling
2–3 tablespoons olive oil
1 large onion, diced
2 cloves garlic, crushed
$1/_2$ teaspoon each sweet paprika, ground
  cardamom, cumin, turmeric and cinnamon
2 medium tomatoes, chopped
10 oz (300 g) canned chickpeas, drained
6 cups (750 g) sliced zucchini, carrots, cauliflower and green beans
2 tablespoons chopped mixed fresh herbs
  such as parsley, mint and fresh coriander
  leaves (cilantro)
$3/_4$ cup (180 ml) vegetable stock

Pistachio Couscous
1 cup (185 g) instant couscous
$1^1/_2$ cups (375 ml) chicken stock
$1/_4$ cup ($1/_2$ stick/60 g) softened butter
$1/_2$ cup (60 g) pistachios, toasted and chopped
Fresh parsley, for garnish

Note: Toast the pistachios by removing the shells and place them under a broiler (grill) or in a frying pan over medium heat and cook, stirring, until they just change color, 3–4 minutes. Be careful not to burn them.

1 Sprinkle the eggplant with salt and let stand for 30 minutes. Rinse under cold water, drain, and pat dry with paper towels.
2 Make the Pistachio Couscous by heating the stock in a small saucepan. Remove from the heat, and stir in the couscous. Let stand until all the liquid is absorbed, 4–5 minutes. Stir in the butter to evenly coat the couscous. Break up any lumps, and spread the couscous out in a bamboo steamer or steamer basket lined with parchment (baking) paper. Cover and steam for 10–15 minutes to heat through. Stir in the pistachios.
3 Heat the oil in a large saucepan and stir-fry the eggplant, onion and garlic until the onion is softened but not brown, about 5 minutes. Add the remaining ingredients to the pan, cover and simmer until the vegetables are tender and flavors well blended, 20–25 minutes.
4 Serve the Couscous topped with the mixed vegetables and garnished with parsley.

Serves 4–6

Meat and Poultry

Beef, veal, pork, lamb and chicken cook quickly when steamed, so tougher cuts of meat are not suitable. Leave meat in a covered steamer for about 5–10 minutes after cooking to allow juices to settle, making the meat tender and juicy.

Steamed meat and poultry will generally be colorless. If preferred, whole chickens and legs of lamb can be browned under the broiler (grill) before serving.

Roasts or whole chickens are large and will swell a little during cooking. As a solution you can place another bamboo steamer or steamer basket upside down over the top, then cover with a lid.

To steam a complete meal, cook rice, pasta or potatoes in the liquid while meat is steaming above it.

Always remember to check for doneness after the minimum suggested time.

General Guide for Steaming Times

Poultry: Very small chicken or Cornish game hen (12 oz–1 1b/350–500 g), 30–40 minutes; whole chicken (3–4 lbs/1.5–1.75 kg), 50–65 minutes; boneless chicken breasts, 12–15 minutes; chicken legs, 15–20 minutes; chicken drumsticks, 12–15 minutes (allow 10–15 minutes extra cooking time for whole chickens with stuffing, 5 minutes extra for stuffed chicken pieces)

Meat: Cooking times will vary depending on preference for rare, medium or well-done meat. If meat is cooked over sliced vegetables, such as potatoes, cooking time will be longer. Beef roasts, 10–12 minutes per pound (500 g), plus an extra 10–15 minutes; thinly sliced steak (sirloin), 3 minutes for medium rare (allow extra cooking time if steaks are rolled with filling); leg of lamb, 15 minutes per pound (500 g), plus an extra 10–15 minutes; chops, 10–15 minutes; porkchops (average-sized), 15–18 minutes.

Spicy Meatballs with Noodles (see recipe on page 69)

Veal Rolls with Pesto and Sun-dried Tomatoes

Whether enjoyed in the summer months, when fresh basil is at its peak, or during the winter, when the intense flavor of sun-dried tomatoes brightens everyone's day, these beautiful rolls make an elegant and impressive meal. Serve them with a simple side of steamed rice or Garlic Mashed Potatoes.

4 veal fillets, about 5 oz (150 g) each, cut in half to make 8 thin sheets
$1/2$ cup (125 g) oil-packed sun-dried tomatoes, drained
12–16 large spinach leaves
8 oz (250 g) fresh mushrooms, stems removed, caps sliced

Basil Pesto
1 cup (30 g) fresh basil leaves
$1/3$ cup (60 g) toasted pine nuts (see note)
$1/2$ cup (60 g) grated Parmesan
2 cloves garlic, crushed
Salt and pepper to taste
$1/2$ cup (125 ml) olive oil
Skewers and toothpicks

Serves 4

1 To make the Basil Pesto, place the basil, pine nuts, Parmesan, garlic, salt, pepper and half of the olive oil in a food processor, and process until smooth. With the machine running, gradually pour in the remaining oil in a thin stream.

2 Pound the veal with a meat mallet until very thin, and lay the sheets flat on a clean work surface. Spread the Basil Pesto over two-thirds of each piece, and place 3 or 4 sun-dried tomatoes at one end. Roll the veal up and secure with a toothpick or skewer at a 45-degree angle. Hold each spinach leaf with tongs and plunge them into boiling water just to soften, 2–3 seconds. Drain. Remove the toothpick and wrap 1 leaf around each veal roll, overlapping 2 leaves if necessary. Secure the toothpick again. Put the mushrooms in a bamboo steamer or steamer basket lined with parchment (baking) paper, with the veal on top.

3 Partially fill a wok or pot with water (steamer should not touch the water) and bring to a rapid boil. Place the steamer over the water, cover and steam until just cooked through, 10–15 minutes. Remove the toothpick.

4 Serve the veal whole or cut diagonally, with cut side up to reveal colorful center. Serve with mushrooms and Garlic Mashed Potatoes (page 41) or steamed rice.

Note: Toast the pine nuts by placing them under a broiler (grill) or in a dry pan over medium heat and cook, stirring, until they just change color, 3–4 minutes. Be careful not to burn them.

Marsala Chicken with Ginger and Mango

The delicious flavor of Marsala Chicken, a popular Italian dish named for that nation's most famous fortified wine, is the inspiration for this festive east-meets-west recipe. Marsala adds a sweet distinctive flavor that is balanced with the pungent and bright flavors of fresh ginger and mango.

8 boneless, skinless chicken thighs
$1/_2$ cup (125 ml) sweet Marsala wine
1 teaspoon five spice powder
1 clove garlic, crushed
1 tablespoon grated fresh ginger
1 mango, peeled and sliced
2 green onions (scallions), cut into $1^1/_2$-inch
  (4-cm) lengths
$1/_3$ cup (40 g) toasted pecans, coarsely
  chopped
16 toothpicks
16 large spinach leaves
$1^1/_2$ lbs (700 g) baby new potatoes

Marsala Sauce
2 tablespoons butter or oil
1 clove garlic, crushed
2 tablespoons all-purpose (plain) flour
1 cup (250 ml) chicken stock
Reserved Marsala marinade

1 Remove any excess fat from the chicken. Put each chicken thigh between a double layer of plastic wrap and pound with a meat mallet until it is the same thickness all over. Combine the wine, five spice, garlic and ginger. Pour it over the chicken and refrigerate for at least 2 hours, or overnight. Turn the chicken at least once.

2 Drain the chicken, reserving the marinade, and lay the pieces flat on a clean work surface. Put 2 or 3 slices of mango, $1/_4$ green onion and 1 tablespoon pecans on one end of each piece of chicken. Roll the meat over to enclose the filling, and skewer closed at a 45-degree angle with 2 toothpicks. Hold each spinach leaf with tongs and quickly plunge it into boiling water until just softened, 2–3 seconds. Drain. Lay 4 leaves out flat on a clean work surface. Place one chicken piece on each leaf, remove the toothpicks. Cover with another leaf, and wrap them around the chicken to enclose. Replace the toothpicks. Place the wrapped chicken on individual pieces of parchment (baking) paper in the steamer.

3 Partially fill a wok or pot with water (steamer should not touch the water) and bring to a rapid boil. Add the potatoes to the water. Place the steamer on top, cover and steam until the potatoes and chicken are cooked (juices run clear when a skewer is inserted), 15–20 minutes.

4 Meanwhile, make the Marsala Sauce. Melt the butter in a small saucepan over medium heat and cook the garlic for 1–2 minutes without browning. Add the flour and cook, stirring constantly, until golden brown. Remove from the heat and stir in the chicken stock and reserved Marsala marinade. Return to the heat and simmer until the mixture thickens.

5 Slice the rolls in half. Serve with the potatoes, remaining sliced mango and Marsala Sauce.

Serves 4

Cordon Bleu Chicken with Avocado and Walnuts

Famous recipes, like this rightly named "blue ribbon" chicken dish, always satisfy when made from scratch with good quality ingredients. The traditional Cordon Bleu is made with Swiss cheese, preferably Gruyère, and prosciutto or another ham. In this recipe, the bold flavor of blue cheese is paired with creamy rich avocado slices.

4 boneless, skinless chicken breasts
8 thin slices blue or Gorgonzola cheese, about $1/4$ inch (6 mm) thick
1 ripe avocado, peeled, pitted and sliced
2 green onions (scallions), chopped
$1/4$ cup (30 g) chopped walnuts
1 bunch fresh lemon thyme or thyme

Fresh Tomato Sauce
3 large tomatoes, peeled and diced
1 tablespoon olive oil
2 green onions (scallions), chopped
1 clove garlic, crushed
2 teaspoons soy sauce
1 tablespoon lemon juice
2 teaspoons Worcestershire sauce
1 tablespoon chopped fresh basil or thyme
Salt and cracked black pepper to taste

Serves 4

1 Cut a slit along one side of each chicken breast to make a pocket. Lay 2 slices cheese, 2 slices avocado, $1/4$ stalk green onion and nuts in each pocket. Skewer closed with a toothpick. Lay half the thyme in a bamboo steamer or steamer basket, with the chicken on top. Spread the remaining thyme over the chicken.
2 Partially fill a wok or pot with water (steamer should not touch the water) and bring to a rapid boil. Place the steamer over the water, cover and steam until cooked, 15–20 minutes (juices run clear when a skewer is inserted in the chicken).
3 To make the Fresh Tomato Sauce, peel the tomatoes by making a cut just through the skin around the center of each tomato. Plunge the tomatoes into boiling water for 1 minute and immediately transfer to cold water. Peel the skins off. Heat the oil in a medium saucepan over medium-low heat. Add the green onions and garlic and cook until soft but not brown, about 5 minutes. Reduce the heat, stir in the remaining ingredients, cover and cook until thick, about 10 minutes. If a thinner sauce is preferred, add a little chicken stock.
4 Spoon the Fresh Tomato Sauce over the chicken or in individual serving bowls as shown, sprinkle the chicken with sprigs of fresh lemon thyme, and serve with steamed rice or baby new potatoes.

Note: For an interesting variation, cook the chicken on thickly sliced fennel or spinach and serve that as a side dish. Or gently boil $1^1/4$ lbs (600 g) baby new potatoes in liquid while the chicken is steaming above.

Pork Chops with Honey Sauce and Pear

Bursting with flavor, this dish proves that steaming is suitable for all types of cooking and tastes—even for meat lovers! Marinated in a rich combination of soy sauce, honey and sherry, and then flavored with mustard and fresh herbs while steaming, these chops are so delicious they may become a regular staple in your home.

3 tablespoons soy sauce

3 tablespoons honey

3 tablespoons dry sherry

4 pork chops, trimmed

4 teaspoons mustard seeds

1 firm pear, peeled, cored, and sliced into thin pieces

3–4 potatoes, sliced into $1/4$-inch (6-mm) rounds

2 yams or sweet potatoes, cut into $1/4$-inch (6-mm) rounds

2 red onions, sliced into $1/4$-inch (6-mm) rounds

2 tablespoons olive oil

2 tablespoons chopped fresh herbs such as sage, parsley, thyme or rosemary

Salt and freshly ground black pepper, to taste

2 tablespoons chopped fresh parsley, for garnish (optional)

1 Mix the soy sauce, honey and wine or sherry, and pour it over the pork chops. Cover and marinate for 1–2 hours, turning once. Drain, reserving the marinade.

2 Spread 1 teaspoon of the mustard seeds evenly over the top of each pork chop. Arrange the pear slices diagonally across each chop. In a bowl, toss the diced potatoes, yams and onions with the oil, herbs, salt and pepper, and spread the mixture evenly in a 12-inch (30-cm) bamboo steamer or steamer basket, with the pork chops on top. It does not matter if the potatoes and onions overlap, but leave a small gap between the potatoes and the edge of the steamer basket to allow steam to circulate efficiently.

3 Partially fill a wok or pot with water (steamer should not touch the water) and bring to a rapid boil. Place the steamer over the water, cover and steam until the chops and potatoes are cooked, 20–25 minutes depending on the thickness. If the chops cook through before the potatoes, simply remove and keep warm while continuing to cook the potatoes. Cook the marinade in a small saucepan. Serve the pork with the hot marinade, yams, and potatoes sprinkled with fresh parsley.

Note: Steam green beans in a second steamer basket for the last 10–12 minutes of cooking time and serve as a side dish.

Serves 4

Steamed Whole Chicken with Herb Stuffing

A steamed whole chicken is rich in flavor, succulent and moist—the perfect dish for a leisurely Sunday dinner.

2 cups (375 g) instant couscous or instant
 wild rice
1$^1/_2$ cups (375 ml) boiling water or stock
$^3/_4$ cup (1$^1/_2$ sticks/180 g) softened butter
2 cloves garlic, crushed
2 green onions (scallions), finely chopped
2 teaspoons cumin seeds
Pinch of ground saffron
$^1/_4$ cup (10 g) chopped fresh coriander
 leaves (cilantro)
1$^1/_4$ cups (250 g) mixed dried raisins, dates
 and apricots
$^1/_2$ cup (75 g) pine nuts, toasted
$^1/_4$ cup (10 g) chopped fresh parsley
$^1/_2$ cup (75 g) slivered almonds, toasted
1 chicken, about 3$^1/_2$ lbs (1.8 kg)

Sherry Sauce
1 cup (250 ml) chicken stock
$^1/_4$ cup (60 ml) dry sherry or Madeira
1$^1/_3$ tablespoons cornstarch
2 teaspoons water

1 Put the instant couscous or wild rice in a medium bowl and pour the boiling water over it. Let stand until all the water is absorbed, 4–5 minutes. Heat the butter in a small pan. Add the garlic, green onions, cumin and saffron, and cook until fragrant, about 1 minute. Pour over the couscous, mixing well. Stir in the remaining ingredients and lightly pack into the chicken. Close the flap and secure with a skewer or toothpick. Put the chicken in a bamboo steamer or steamer basket lined with lemon or lime leaves. If the chicken is too high, turn another steamer upside down over it and then cover with a lid or greased foil.
2 Partially fill a wok or pot with water (steamer should not touch the water) and bring to a rapid boil. Place the remaining couscous or rice into oiled heat-proof bowls and steam with the chicken. Let stand for 2 minutes before unmolding. Place the steamer over the water, cover and steam until the chicken is cooked, 1$^1/_4$–1$^1/_2$ hours, or until the juices run clear when a skewer is inserted into the chicken thigh.
3 Make the Sherry Sauce by heating the stock and sherry in a small saucepan. Mix the cornstarch and water, then add 1 tablespoon of hot stock. Stir into the remaining stock and cook, stirring, until thick.
4 Serve the chicken with the Sherry Sauce on the side and the remaining couscous or rice as an accompaniment to the chicken.

Note: Toast the pinenuts or almonds by placing the nuts under a broiler (grill) or in a dry pan over medium heat, stirring until they just change color, 3–4 minutes. Be careful not to burn them. For an appetizing variation, the chicken can be browned under a broiler (grill) if desired, before serving with the Sherry Sauce.

Serves 4–5

Spicy Meatballs with Noodles

Tender meatballs are the ultimate comfort food, and when spiced are sure to heat up a cold winter day! For added heat, spice up the sauce to your liking. Enjoy the meatballs and sauce over fresh Italian pasta of your choice or, for an east-west experience, try meaty udon noodles (shown at the bottom, left of page 68).

1 lb (500 g) ground beef
1 large onion, finely chopped
1 clove garlic, crushed
2$^1/_2$ tablespoons tomato paste
2 tablespoons Worcestershire sauce
2 tablespoons chopped fresh parsley
1 finger-length red chili pepper, deseeded
 and finely chopped
1 egg, lightly beaten
Salt and freshly ground pepper
1$^1/_2$ lbs (700 g) fresh pasta or udon noodles
$^1/_4$ teaspoon salt
2 tablespoons olive oil
2 tablespoons chopped fresh parsley, for
 garnish

Spicy Tomato Sauce
Fresh Tomato Sauce (page 63)
1 finger-length red chili pepper, deseeded
 and finely chopped (optional)

Note: For a delicious variation, toss the meatballs in Basil Pesto (see page 59) instead of the above Sauce.

1 Combine the beef, onion, garlic, tomato paste, Worcestershire sauce, parsley, chili pepper, egg, salt and pepper in a medium bowl, mixing well. Line a large bamboo steamer or steamer basket with parchment (baking) paper. With wet hands, take about 1 tablespoon of the mixture at a time and shape it into small balls, and place in a single layer in the steamer.
2 Partially fill a wok or pot with water (steamer should not touch the water) and bring to a rapid boil. Place the steamer over the water, cover and steam until the meatballs are cooked, 8–10 minutes. Add the noodles and salt to the water for the last 6 minutes of cooking, or until just tender. Drain the noodles and toss with the olive oil to keep them from sticking.
3 While the meatballs are cooking, make the Spicy Tomato Sauce by heating the Fresh Tomato Sauce in a small saucepan, adding the chili pepper if desired. Divide the noodles among 4 plates and serve topped with meatballs and Sauce, and sprinkled with parsley.

Serves 4

Seafood

There is nothing quite as succulent and flavorsome as steamed seafood. However, it cooks surprisingly quickly, and so is very easy to overcook. Check at the minimum cooking time, because you can always cook it for a little longer if necessary. For added flavor, marinate before steaming, then reduce the marinade and serve as a sauce.

Do not be limited by the seafood suggested in each recipe. In many cases, seafood types are interchangeable—only the cooking times may vary slightly. Cooking a large whole fish may be a problem without a fish kettle, so you may have to settle for two smaller fish that fit your bamboo steamer or steamer basket. Otherwise, try fish steaks, cutlets or fillets. Steaming time is dictated more by the thickness of the fish than its weight. In general, fish is cooked 8–10 minutes per inch (4–5 minutes per $\frac{1}{2}$ inch). To test if it's cooked, insert a fork into the thickest part of the fish. If the flesh is opaque throughout and flakes easily, it's done. If the seafood is stuffed, wrapped, or cooked in a two-level steamer, allow extra cooking time and rotate the levels of the steamer halfway through for even cooking.

General Guide for Steaming Times (depending on size)

Whole fish: 10–15 minutes per lb (500 g)
Fish fillets: 5–8 minutes
Fish cutlets: 8–12 minutes
Mussels: 3–6 minutes
Prawns: 3–6 minutes
Scallops: 2–3 minutes
Lobster: 10–15 minutes

Spicy Shrimp with Chinese Noodles
(see recipe on page 76)

Thai Fish Curry

This delicious curry recipe is deceptively quick to prepare, making it perfect for a weekday dinner, yet suitably elegant for a special evening or when entertaining. If you pefer a mild curry, use less curry paste or try yellow curry paste, which is the most mild of the Thai curries.

2–3 large banana leaves or aluminum foil, cut into six 6-inch (15-cm) rounds
1 lb (500 g) white fish fillets, finely sliced
2 tablespoons Thai red or green curry paste (available from Asian food stores)
1 tablespoon chopped roasted peanuts
1 cup (250 ml) thick coconut cream
2 eggs, lightly beaten
1 tablespoon fish sauce
Salt and pepper to taste
1 cup (90 g) Chinese cabbage leaves, finely shredded
2 tablespoons thick coconut cream, for garnish (optional)
1 finger-length red chili pepper, deseeded and thinly sliced for garnish (optional)

1 Blanch the banana leaf rounds in hot water to soften, 30–60 seconds. Drain and pat dry with paper towels. Fold each round into a wide cone and staple, then place in a round or square heat-proof bowl, or use the rounds to line oiled rice bowls.
2 Partially fill a wok or pot with water (steamer should not touch the water) and bring to a rapid boil. Mix the fish, curry paste, peanuts, coconut cream, eggs, fish sauce, salt and pepper in a large bowl. Divide into 6 portions. Divide the shredded cabbage into 6 portions.
3 Fill each banana cup with 1 portion fish mixture, then 1 portion shredded cabbage, and place them in a bamboo steamer or steamer basket. Cover with double layer of greased plastic wrap or parchment (baking) paper, or place a cloth under the lid to stop any condensation from dripping onto the cups. Place the steamer over the water, cover and steam until set, 10–15 minutes. (A skewer inserted into custard will come out clean when cooked.) Garnish with a dollop of coconut cream and sliced chili pepper if desired. Serve hot.

Serves 6

Shrimp, Chicken and Mushroom Egg Custard

In this delicious version of a steamed Japanese egg custard cup, known as *chawan mushi*, all of the subtle nuances of Japanese cuisine are retained in this mild, understated dish. These rich egg custard cups make a satisfying meal, or they can also be served as a first course in a larger meal.

4 dried black Chinese mushrooms
5 oz (150 g) skinless, boneless chicken breast, diced
1 teaspoon soy sauce
1 teaspoon sake, Shaoxing rice wine or dry white wine
8 medium shrimp, shelled and deveined
$1/2$ cup (60 g) sliced carrot, halved
4 spinach leaves, blanched and chopped
4 eggs
Thinly sliced lime or lemon rind, for garnish

Broth
$2^1/_2$ cups (625 ml) Japanese dashi stock (bonito stock, see note)
2 teaspoons soy sauce
1 tablespoon sake, Shaoxing rice wine or dry white wine
Pinch of salt

1 Soak the mushrooms in warm water for 20 minutes. Drain, gently squeezing to remove the excess water. (Do not discard the water; it will make a good addition to any stock.) Discard the stems, and chop each mushroom cap into 2 or 3 pieces.
2 Marinate the chicken in the soy sauce and sake for 10 minutes.
3 Make the Broth by mixing the dashi stock, soy sauce, sake and salt in a small bowl, stirring until the salt dissolves. Divide the mushrooms, chicken, shrimp, carrot and spinach among 4–6 cups or heat-proof bowls. Lightly beat the eggs, but do not allow it to become frothy. Stir in the Broth, mixing well. Pour the egg and Broth mixture into each cup and garnish with the lime or lemon rind. Cover with a double layer of plastic wrap or place a cloth under the lid when covering to stop condensation from dripping onto the custards. Place the cups in a large bamboo steamer or steamer basket, and cover.
4 Partially fill a wok or pot with water (steamer should not touch the water) and bring to a rapid boil. Place the steamer over the water, cover and steam until the custard has just set, 15–20 minutes. (A skewer inserted into custard will come out clean when custard is cooked. This custard does not set very firmly and is still quite liquid when cooked.)

Note: To make instant dashi stock (bonito stock), combine $2^1/_2$ cups (625 ml) boiling hot water with 1 teaspoon dashi granules, stirring, until the granules dissolve.

Makes 4–6

Spicy Shrimp with Chinese Noodles

This zesty flavor-packed dish with fresh herbs and balsamic vinegar is a favorite in my household.

2 lbs (1 kg) fresh jumbo shrimp, shelled and deveined
1 tablespoon olive oil
2 cloves garlic, crushed
1 leek, white part only, sliced and washed
1 small bell pepper, deseeded and diced
2 tablespoons tomato paste
3 large tomatoes, skinned and diced
2 teaspoons balsamic vinegar
1 tablespoon chopped fresh basil
1 tablespoon chopped fresh oregano
$^1/_2$ cup (125 ml) dry white wine
1 lb (500 g) fresh yellow wheat noodles or fettuccine

1 Put the shrimp in a large steamer basket and cover. Heat the olive oil in a large saucepan slightly larger in diameter than steamer. Stir-fry the garlic and leek for 2–3 minutes, without browning. Add the pepper and tomato paste and cook until the paste starts to darken and becomes aromatic, 2–3 minutes. Add the rest of the ingredients, except the noodles. Place the steamer over the pan and steam until the shrimp turn pink, 3–6 minutes. Remove the shrimp from the heat and continue to simmer the sauce if a thicker sauce is preferred.

2 Cover the noodles with hot water for 1–2 minutes. Drain and separate with a fork, and place in a large bowl. Stir in the sauce and shrimp. Serve with a good red wine.

Serves 4

Fresh Salmon Salad with Soy Ginger Dressing

Celebrate the arrival of summer with this elegant salmon salad made with tender peas and asparagus.

1 lb (500 g) boneless salmon
1 cup (100 g) sugar snap peas
4 asparagus stalks, cut into thirds
1 cup (100 g) snow pea or soybean sprouts
$1/4$ cup (15 g) fresh coriander leaves (cilantro)
1 baby cucumber, thinly sliced

Soy Ginger Dressing
2 tablespoons soy sauce
2 teaspoons rice vinegar or white wine vinegar
2 tablespoons sesame oil
1 teaspoon grated fresh ginger

Serves 2

1 Steam the salmon, covered, over boiling water for 10 minutes. Remove the skin and flake into large pieces. Blanch the snap peas and asparagus in boiling water for 1 minute. Drain and refresh under cold water. Drain well. Mix with remaining ingredients.
2 Whisk together the Soy Ginger Dressing ingredients. Pour it over the vegetables and toss. Transfer to serving plates and pile the salmon on top.

Note: Use a bamboo steamer inside a larger saucepan to steam the salmon. You can microwave the asparagus and snap peas or place them in the steamer after cooking the salmon. If sugar snap peas aren't available, you can substitute snow peas. Do not overcook the salmon; it is best when just barely cooked!

Whole Snapper with a Tangy Orange Sauce

Fish is at its most flavorful when prepared whole, and its presentation the most dramatic. In addition, whole fish provides extra clues for checking freshness. When buying whole fresh fish, along with checking for a fresh aroma and firm texture, look for bright, clear full eyes (cloudy or sunken eyes indicate stale fish).

1 tablespoon soy sauce

Juice and grated rind of 1 orange

4 small whole snapper or trout, 8–12 oz
  (250–350 g) each

1 tablespoon butter

1 large leek, washed and thinly sliced, green
  tops reserved

1 clove garlic, crushed

2 oranges, sliced

$^1/_2$ cup (75 g) hazelnuts, toasted and
  coarsely chopped, for garnish (see note)

2 tablespoons chopped fresh parsley, for
  garnish

Tangy Orange Sauce

$^1/_3$ cup (80 ml) orange marmalade

1 tablespoon soy sauce

2 teaspoons water

Serves 4

1 Mix the soy sauce, orange juice and rind in a small bowl. Pour over the fish in a flat dish. Allow to marinate for 30 minutes, turning once. Meanwhile, melt the butter in a medium pan over medium heat and stir-fry the leek and garlic until softened but not browned, 3–4 minutes. Let cool.

2 Make 3 diagonal slashes on each side of the fish for even cooking. Fill the fish cavities with the fried leeks. Lay 1 or 2 overlapped green leek tops on a clean work surface for each fish. Top with half the orange slices, then the fish. Scatter the remaining orange slices on top. Place 2 fish in each level of a large 12-inch (30-cm) two-level steamer, and cover.

3 Partially fill a large wok or pot with water (steamer should not touch the water) and bring to a rapid boil. Place the two-level steamers over the water and steam until the fish flakes when tested with a fork and the flesh is opaque, 10–12 minutes, depending on thickness. Rotate the levels of the steamer halfway through for even cooking.

4 Meanwhile, make the Tangy Orange Sauce by heating the marmalade, soy sauce and water in a small saucepan.

5 Place the fish on serving plates and discard the orange slices. Pour the hot Tangy Orange Sauce over the top and garnish with hazelnuts and chopped parsley.

Note: Toast the hazelnuts in a preheated oven 350°F (180°C) for 8–10 minutes. Fold in a kitchen towel and rub together to remove skins.

Calamari Rings with Sweet Lime Dressing

One of the quickest-cooking sources of protein available, calamari is the perfect choice for when you need to get dinner on the table fast. In fact, the greatest challenge to preparing calamari is to not over cook it, which causes its tender texture to become rubbery. Served over a bed of greens, these delicious calamari are a great meal-in-one.

1 lb (500 g) fresh calamari (squid) tubes, cleaned and sliced $1/2$ inch (12 mm) thick
$2^1/_2$ tablespoons fresh lemon juice
2 cloves garlic, crushed
1 finger-length red chili pepper, deseeded and finely chopped
2 tablespoons fish sauce
$2^1/_2$ tablespoons fresh lime juice
1 tablespoon shaved palm sugar or dark brown sugar
$1/_2$ teaspoon sesame oil
2 green onions (scallions), finely chopped
1 English (hothouse) cucumber, deseeded and chopped
$1/_4$ cup (10 g) chopped fresh coriander leaves (cilantro)
$1/_4$ cup (10 g) chopped fresh mint leaves
3 cups (90 g) mixed green salad
2 tablespoons Fried Garlic Chips (see note)

1 Place the calamari in a bowl with the lemon juice, garlic and half of the chopped chili pepper, and allow to marinate for 30 minutes. Drain. Place the calamari in a bamboo steamer or steamer basket.
2 Partially fill a wok or pot with water (steamer should not touch the water) and bring to a rapid boil. Place the steamer over the water, cover and steam until the calamari is opaque, 3–4 minutes. Remove from the steamer and let cool.
3 Combine the rest of the chopped chili pepper with the fish sauce, lime juice, palm sugar and sesame oil in a small bowl, stirring until the sugar dissolves. Combine the calamari, green onions, cucumber, coriander and mint leaves in another bowl and add the dressing mixture. Toss to mix well. Arrange on salad leaves, garnished with fried garlic chips.

Note: Make the Fried Garlic Chips by heating 1 cup (250 ml) oil in a small saucepan over medium heat and fry 10–15 thinly sliced cloves garlic until golden brown and crisp, 2–3 minutes. Be careful not to burn. Fried Garlic Chips can be made ahead and stored in an airtight container.

Serves 4

Steamed Fish Japanese Style

In this simple recipe marinated fresh fish is wrapped in a beautiful Zenlike package that is sure to beguile everyone at your table. Easy to prepare, this wholesome yet elegant meal is suitable for quick weekday dinners or when you want something special to impress your guests.

$^1/_4$ cup (60 ml) Shaoxing rice wine, sake or dry sherry

$^1/_4$ cup (60 ml) soy sauce

1 tablespoon fish sauce

1 teaspoon sesame oil

4 fresh fish fillets (snapper, bream, perch, salmon), about 7 oz (200 g) each, and 5 inches (13 cm) long

8 green onions (scallions)

4 sheets toasted nori (yaki-nori or toasted seaweed)

$^1/_2$ red bell pepper, deseeded and thinly sliced

3 tablespoons Japanese Pickled Ginger (purchased)

1 Mix the wine or sherry, soy sauce, fish sauce and sesame oil in a bowl, and pour it over the fish fillets in a flat dish. Allow to marinate for 20–30 minutes, turning once. Drain, discarding the marinade.
2 Cut the green onions into same length as the fish fillets. Lay each fillet diagonally across a sheet of nori. If the nori is too big for the fillets, trim to smaller square shape. Place 2 or 3 strips of bell pepper and slices of Japanese Pickled Ginger down the center of the fish fillet. Add 2 stalk green onions, with one green tip and one white tip at each end. Lightly brush each side flap of the nori with water, fold both sides over the fish towards the center, pressing gently to seal. The fish and vegetable strips will still be visible at either end. Place 2 fish fillets in each steamer basket, and cover.
3 Partially fill a wok or pot with water (steamer should not touch the water) and bring to a rapid boil. Place the steamer over the water, cover and steam until the fish flakes when tested with fork and the flesh is opaque, 5–8 minutes, depending on the thickness of the fillets. Switch the steamer levels halfway through for even cooking. Remove the fish from the steamer and serve with the remaining Japanese Pickled Ginger and steamed rice.

Serves 4

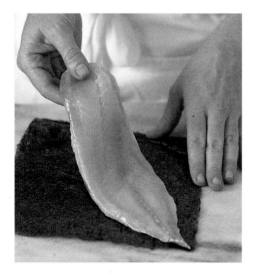

Desserts

It is surprising how many desserts can be prepared by steaming—steamed puddings to cakes, velvety custards and créme brûlée, mousses, rice pudding and even poached fruit or fresh fruit kabobs. For optimum flavor, serve with fresh flavored cream or yogurt, ice cream, custard or wine sauces.

Preparation is very simple: cook in a covered steamer over rapidly simmering water, or directly in the pot with rapidly simmering water halfway up the sides of the dishes. Many such desserts can be prepared ahead and refrigerated until required.

A two-level steamer can be used to prepare a sauce at the same time as the dessert, or the dessert at the same time as the main course. If the dessert is covered (with aluminum foil for example), the flavors of the dessert and main course will not mix. Steamed desserts are simple and delicious!

Remember to pleat the parchment (baking) paper before covering puddings to allow for expansion, and to place a kitchen towel under the lid to absorb any condensation before it drips onto the food. Pleating parchment (baking) paper is simply putting a pleat in the paper before placing it over the food that is to be steamed. This allows food to expand and prevents it from being squashed by the paper when it expands.

When using ramekins, tie a piece of string with a loop around the rim of ramekins, especially if using a deep pot, for easy removal of hot dishes without burning yourself. The ramekins called for in this section are 8 oz (250 ml) in capacity and they can be substituted with medium-sized Chinese teacups. Using Chinese teacups is great for serving at large parties and gatherings.

Grand Marnier Crème Caramel (see recipe on page 93)

Hot Mocha and Brandied Raisin Soufflé

When most of us think of a soufflé, we think of something that is savory and served warm. But soufflés can be savory or sweet, hot or cold, and in this case steamed. In this soufflé the complex flavors of coffee, brandy-soaked raisins and dark chocolate combine to create a very adult dessert. Don't waste this one on the kiddies!

4 oz (125 g) dark chocolate
$^1/_4$ cup (60 g) superfine (caster) sugar
4 eggs, separated and 1 extra egg white
1 teaspoon instant coffee granules

Brandied Raisins
$^1/_3$ cup (60 g) raisins
1 cup (250 ml) brandy

Makes 6 small soufflés or 1 large soufflé

1 Make the Brandied Raisins by placing the raisins in an airtight jar and cover with brandy. Cover the jar and soak overnight.
2 Lightly butter six 1-cup (250-ml) ramekins or one 6-cup (1$^1/_2$ liter) soufflé dish. Put the chocolate in a bowl and place the bowl in a bamboo steamer or steamer basket. Place uncovered, over a wok or pot of simmering water, to melt the chocolate. Remove from the heat and add the sugar, stirring until dissolved. Lightly beat 4 egg yolks and the coffee granules. Stir into the chocolate, mixing gently. In a large bowl, beat the 5 egg whites until stiff, glossy peaks form. Stir one-third of the egg whites into the chocolate mixture, then lightly fold in the remaining whites. Drain the Brandied Raisins and divide them among the prepared ramekins. Spoon the chocolate mixture over the Raisins. Cover each ramekin with a piece of buttered parchment (baking) paper or buttered plastic wrap.
3 Partially fill a 12-inch (30-cm) wok or pot with water (steamer should not touch the water) and bring to a rapid boil. Arrange the ramekins on both levels of a two-level steamer, or place a large soufflé dish on one level. Place over the water, cover and steam until set, 12–15 minutes (switch levels halfway through for even cooking), although the soufflé will still be slightly sticky inside. Serve immediately, or refrigerate and serve chilled.

Note: Use Chinese teacups instead of ramekins to make smaller individual soufflés. If they do not all fit in steamer either use two stacked steamers, rotating halfway through for even cooking or whisk half the egg whites and cook half the mixture at a time.

Lemon, Date and Walnut Cake

This simple nut cake is a great all-purpose sweet. It's a perfect afternoon accompaniment with a tea or coffee break or, when served with fresh fruit or fruit coulis and fresh cream, is transformed into an elegant after dinner dessert.

4 eggs
$^2/_3$ cup (150 g) sugar
2 teaspoons grated lemon rind
1 cup (150 g) all-purpose (plain) flour, sifted
2 tablespoons coarsely chopped walnuts
2 tablespoons coarsely chopped dates
$^1/_2$ teaspoon ground cinnamon

Makes one 9-inch square cake

1 Put the eggs in a bowl and beat them until frothy, about 2 minutes. Add half of the sugar and beat until light and fluffy, 2–3 minutes. Add the remaining sugar and lemon rind and beat for 10 minutes.

2 Gradually stir the flour into the egg mixture. Do not add too quickly, or the flour will sink. Grease a 9-inch (23-cm) square pan, and spoon in half the mixture. Sprinkle with half the nuts and dates and carefully spoon in the remaining egg mixture. Sprinkle the top with the remaining nuts and dates, then the cinnamon. Cover the pan loosely, to allow for rising, with a double layer of greased plastic wrap or parchment (baking) paper, or place a kitchen towel under the steamer lid to keep any condensation from falling on the cake. Place in a large steamer and cover.

3 Partially fill a wok or pot with water (steamer should not touch the water) and bring to a rapid boil. Place the steamer over the water, cover and steam until a skewer inserted in the cake comes out cleanly, about 15 minutes. Cut the cake into squares or slices and serve warm or cold with fresh fruit or fruit coulis and whipped cream.

Creamy Coconut Black Rice Pudding

In Southeast Asia, where the rich nutty flavor of sticky black rice is particularly popular, delicious black rice pudding is enjoyed for breakfast and dessert.

1 cup (220 g) uncooked black glutinous rice
1 cup (250 ml) cold water
1¹/₂ cups (375 ml) coconut milk
¹/₃ cup (60 g) shaved palm sugar or dark
  brown sugar
2 teaspoons grated lime or lemon rind
Pinch of salt
1 cup (250 ml) thick coconut cream (optional)
1 mango, peeled and sliced (optional)

Serves 4–6

1 Place the rice in a bowl and add cold water to cover. Let soak overnight, drain, and rinse well under cold running water. Place the rice and water in a bowl that fits in a bamboo steamer or steamer basket.
2 Partially fill a wok or pot with water (steamer should not touch the water) and bring to a rapid boil. Place the steamer over the water, cover and steam until the rice is tender, 40–45 minutes, stirring occasionally. Remove from the heat and stir in the coconut milk, sugar, lime rind, and salt. Cover and steam until thickened to consistency of hot cereal, 15–20 minutes. Drizzle the thick coconut cream over the top, if desired, and serve with fresh mango slices.

Sweet Rice Cakes with Banana or Mango

In this exotic treat, banana leaves do double duty—serving as a wrapper while simultaneously imparting flavor.

1 cup (220 g) uncooked white glutinous rice

3 tablespoons shaved palm sugar or dark brown sugar

$^3/_4$ cup (180 ml) coconut milk

12 banana leaf squares, about 6 inches (15 cm) across, blanched in hot water to soften

1–2 ripe bananas, peeled and sliced, or 1 large mango

Juice of 1 lime

1 teaspoon grated lime rind

Makes 12 parcels

1 Cover the rice with cold water and let it soak overnight. Drain. Line a bamboo steamer or steamer basket with a cheesecloth and spread the rice evenly on top of the cloth. Steam until the rice is tender, 40–45 minutes, adding more water if required. Remove from the heat.

2 Put the rice in a bowl and stir in the sugar and coconut milk. Place 1 tablespoon of the rice onto the center of each banana leaf square. Lay a slice of banana or mango on the rice with a drop or two of lime juice and a pinch of rind. Fold one end of the banana leaf over the rice, then fold both sides in and roll up so the rice is fully enclosed. Secure with string or toothpicks. Repeat with the remaining rice.

3 Place the parcels in a steamer basket over boiling water, cover, and steam for 15 minutes. Serve whole or halved.

Grand Marnier Crème Caramel

Grand Marnier, an extremely smooth cognac-based orange flavored liqueur, adds upscale elegance to whatever it touches, including this subtle crème caramel. For added decadence, serve your guests a nip of this renowned liqueur as an after dinner drink alongside the crème caramel—a perfect match!

1/3 cup (65 g) sugar
3 tablespoons water
4 eggs
2 tablespoons superfine (caster) sugar
2 1/2 cups (625 ml) milk
1 teaspoon vanilla extract
1 tablespoon Grand Marnier
1 teaspoon grated orange rind

Serves 6

1 Combine the sugar and water in a small saucepan and melt the sugar over low heat, stirring constantly. Increase the heat and boil until the mixture caramelizes to a golden brown color, 4–5 minutes. Be careful not to let it burn. Immediately pour into 6 small ramekins, while tipping each dish to cover the sides with caramel.
2 Beat the eggs and sugar together until well combined. Stir in the milk, vanilla, Grand Marnier and orange rind. Pour the mixture into the ramekins and cover with oiled aluminum foil or a double layer of plastic wrap.
3 Partially fill a 12-inch (30-cm) wok or pot with water (steamer should not touch the water) and bring to a rapid boil. Put the ramekins in 2 stacked bamboo steamers or two-tiered steamer baskets. Place the steamer over the water, cover and steam until the custard has set, about 20 minutes (an inserted skewer will come out clean when the custard is cooked). Switch baskets halfway through for even cooking. Remove from the steamer and cool to room temperature. Cover each dish with a fresh sheet of plastic wrap, and refrigerate until required.
4 To serve, place a plate over each custard and invert it. Serve with fresh berries.

Note: Substitute lemon or lime rind for orange rind.

Mini Christmas Fruitcakes

With this delicious recipe, you can recreate the proud traditions and flavors of holidays yore.

2 lbs (1 kg) dried mixed fruit
1 cup (250 ml) brandy, whiskey or rum
$1/3$ cup (60 g) candied cherries
$1/3$ cup (60 g) candied ginger, chopped
1 cup (220 g) dark brown sugar
1 tablespoon molasses
Grated rind of 1 orange
Grated rind of 1 lemon
4 eggs, lightly beaten
1 cup (2 sticks/250 g) softened butter,
$1^1/_2$ cups (235 g) all-purpose (plain) flour,
  sifted
$1/_2$ cup (75 g) self-raising flour, sifted
2 tablespoons mixed spice powder
6 ramekins or 4 small heatproof bowls

Makes 6 small or 4 medium cakes

1 Grease each ramekin. Cut two rounds of parchment (baking) paper to fit inside the base. Combine the dried fruit and liquor in a bowl and cover tightly with a double layer of plastic wrap. Let soak overnight, stirring once or twice.

2 Place the soaked fruit in a large bowl and add the cherries, ginger, sugar, molasses, orange and lemon rind, and eggs. Mix well and stir in the butter, flour and spices. Spoon the mixture into each ramekin, up to 1 inch (2.5 cm) above rim. Smooth with the back of a spoon. Cut 6 sheets of parchment (baking) paper and aluminum foil, each 12 inches (30 cm) square. Lay the paper over the foil and fold a pleat in the center. Place one piece of paper and foil on top of each cake, pushing the foil over the ramekin to seal, and tie with a string. Make a loop of string for easy removal of the cakes from the saucepan. Add enough hot water to come halfway up the sides of the ramekins and steam until cooked, about 1 hour. Add extra hot water to the saucepan if needed.

3 When the cakes are completely cold, remove from the ramekins, and discard the foil and paper. Place in an oven bag and tie tightly with string, then cover the string with a decorative Christmas ribbon and bow.

Published by Periplus Editions, Ltd.

www.periplus.com

Hardcover ISBN 13: 978-0-7946-0580-3

Distributed by
USA
Tuttle Publishing, 364 Innovation Drive,
North Clarendon, VT 05759-9436.
Tel: (802) 773-8930 Fax: (802) 773-6993
info@tuttlepublishing.com
www.tuttlepublishing.com

Asia Pacific
Berkeley Books Pte Ltd.
61 Tai Seng Avenue
#02-12, Singapore 534167.
Tel: (65) 6280-1330 Fax: (65) 6280-6290
inquiries@periplus.com.sg
www.periplus.com

Printed in Singapore
12 11 10   5 4 3 2